THE MAKING OF

Gypsy

Denise McLaglen

THE MAKING OF

Gypsy

KEITH GAREBIAN

ECW PRESS

CANADIAN CATALOGUING IN PUBLICATION DATA

Garebian, Keith, 1943–
The making of "Gypsy"

(Classic Broadway musicals)
Includes bibliographical references.

ISBN 1-55022-192-2

I. Styne, Jule, 1905–94. Gypsy.
I. Title. II. Series.

ML410.S78G3 1993   782.1'4   C93-094505-0

*The cover picture is of Sandra Curch and Ethel Merman,
courtesy of the New York Public Library for the Perfoming Arts.*

This book has been published with the assistance
of the Ministry of Culture and Communications
of the Province of Ontario, through funds provided
by the Ontario Publishing Centre, and with the assistance
of grants from the Department of Canadian Heritage,
The Canada Council, and the Ontario Arts Council.

Design and imaging by ECW Type & Art, Oakville, Ontario.
Printed by Imprimerie Gagné, Louiseville, Québec.

Distributed by General Distribution Services,
30 Lesmill Road, Toronto, Ontario M3B 2T6.
(416) 445-3333, (800) 387-0172 (Canada), FAX (416) 445-5967.

Distributed to the trade in the United States exclusively
by InBook, 140 Commerce Street, P.O. Box 120261,
East Haven, Connecticut, U.S.A. 06512.
Customer service: (800) 243-0138, FAX (800) 334-3892.

Published by ECW PRESS,
2120 Queen Street East, Suite 200,
Toronto, Ontario M4E 1E2.

For Audrey, Peter, and Elizabeth

TABLE OF CONTENTS

Foreword

THE DIFFICULTY FOR A MODERN STAR in *Gypsy* today is the competition with a ghost — Ethel Merman's, to be exact. It's no longer a case of making the role of Mama Rose credible in all her volcano-force anomalies — of making her seem crazy yet funny, pitiable and savage, sinner and sinned-against. The contradictions are built engagingly into the script. She is downright interesting in her own right and in Arthur Laurents's writing, and only a sub-par actress would fail to capitalize on that interest. However, no matter how skillful in technique, accomplished in singing, deft in comedy, or moving in drama, the modern Mama Rose — be it Angela Lansbury or Tyne Daly or Sandra O'Neill — can never quite muffle the vibrations still echoing from Ethel Merman's vocal cords somewhere above Broadway these thirty-odd years since they first boomed and rattled in the show.

Merman was, perhaps, the most powerful belter on Broadway, but she was by no means the best singer. She frequently had too much vibrato, too many overly stretched vowels, too many pile-driving consonants. She fought any orchestra and won, and only the very best conductors knew how to accompany her and yield gracefully. In her acting, the seams showed all too candidly. Much of her acting was done according to prescribed pattern: this scene for knockabout farce, this one for domestic drama, another for risqué humour, another for heart-tugging poignancy, and then one for a blistering climax.

In a rare retrospective comment, Arthur Laurents once suggested that Merman's performance in *Gypsy* might not have worked in today's theatre. Even considering that theatre people are always most in love with their newest projects and that Laurents was, at the time

9

of the comment, directing a revival of Gypsy with Tyne Daly, his remarks do have a certain truth. Styles change in the theatre — as, indeed, they do elsewhere. What was once considered singularly appropriate and refined in one period might well be thought vulgarly offensive in another.

And yet the thing that probably matters most for audiences is the emotional connection, for passion in a musical has to register at the time of vocal rendition. And that was something Ethel Merman could manage with powerful ease. She belonged to an old tradition of the musical stage — that of plastering emotion onto her role, the scenery, and the boards, but she involved the audience instantly. She came to prominence in an era when musicals had the very limited ambition of being merely happy and of making audiences happy. Musicals did not have much that was sensible or weighty in their plots — if, indeed, they had recognizable plots. And songs did not necessarily have to push plots along. Audiences came to the theatre not so much to see a story as to hear the songs and to gasp at the elaborate production numbers (many of which had no logical connection to the narrative). A musical's book was written to be forgotten — or so it seemed for many decades. And musical stars earned their reputations for being blithe and deft at interrupting the story with numbers. Of course, it was indisputable that many of their songs had memorable lyrics — at least in the cases of the leading stars. And Merman had the help of Irving Berlin, Richard Whiting, Arthur Schwartz, Dorothy Fields, Ira Gershwin, Cole Porter, Lew Brown, and Ray Henderson. In turn, she gave the songs a new fillip and their shows a powerful fizz. No wonder, then, that she was sometimes not merely an "act" but the entire "act"! And for the longest while she made it seem that the real genius of American musical comedy lay in its stars.

In Gypsy she had the triumph of a lifetime, both in singing and acting, and it seemed to all the world who bothered about such things that Gypsy was made especially for Merman.

But time makes revisionists of us all. And in retrospect, it appears that Merman ran away with the legend of the show but not necessarily with the truth — for the truth of the matter is that Merman needed *Gypsy* in order to re-make her own stardom, and that, for all its defects, the play is as integrated a musical as could be expected of the genre up to that point in Broadway history.

Gypsy tells the story of the metamorphosis of young Rose Louise Hovick from clumsy novice vaudevillian to the stylish stripper Gypsy Rose Lee. She is prompted along the way by Mama Rose, an outrageous stage-mother with an audacious instinct for survival. Arthur Laurents's libretto, Jule Styne's music, and Stephen Sondheim's lyrics have become recognizable classics with their collective humour, pathos, and power. For craftsmanship and general entertainment, with some sharp satire worked into the grain, the show is as dazzling today as it first seemed when it premièred in 1959. But Merman and her collaborators discovered all this for themselves. They were ahead of the critics who today must admit that Merman and *Gypsy* compel us to take seriously the idea of art in American musical theatre.

Broadway Mama

WITH ITS ENCHANTING ADVENTURES along the vaudeville and burlesque circuits of the twenties and thirties and its celebration of heroic Mama Rose, an outrageous stage-mother with an audacious instinct for survival, *Gypsy* is in a very fundamental sense fully in the American grain. With brazen humour and spunk it conveys a colourfully textured view of several strata of Americana — the slatternly dressing-rooms and garish stages of peeling vaudeville houses and sleazy strip palaces in which young women submitted themselves to any number of titillating stage acts in order to earn a living and, perhaps, ascend a rather rickety ladder of show-biz. Ostensibly about the metamorphosis of young Rose Louise Hovick from clumsy novice vaudevillian to the stylish ecdysiast Gypsy Rose Lee, it manages to bump her carefully aside in order that her mother, a benevolent demon of ambition, might shine out in her tough, gritty, playful individuality. Almost singlehandedly this character (with something of a rogue-heroine about her) transforms what could have been a low-brow story into high art. In one undeniable sense, she is a larger-than-life representation of American Mom-ism, that syndrome that so bedevils many a generation that feel smothered by the hand that rocks the cradle and tightens the silver cord. Yet, Rose is not grotesque; she is a human being, subject to her own chimeras of pain and travail, who transcends everything because of the hard-earned wisdom of surviving lost loves, poverty, and chaos. When her turn comes to dream for herself, she seizes it with the sort of rough readiness that we, not inappropriately, identify as the essence of American enterprise and opportunism.

As played by Ethel Merman, the role became a classic characterization that swept aside all other characters. Merman, who had flashed across the Broadway stage like a meteor in *Anything Goes* (1934), *Annie Get Your Gun* (1946), and *Call Me Madam* (1950), was now not simply replicating her earlier serio-comic caricatures or brassy heroines. Here, at last, was an unlikable, unreliable, yet stirring female, and as Merman charged up the aisle of the Broadway Theatre, sang about getting and taking, then lured and teased Herbie about managing her plans and future, turned away from Baby June who had eloped as a fourteen-year-old teenager with her boy-lover, and was turned away by Louise who had become a star and wanted a life of her own, she never lost her ferocious dedication to herself. Friendship and love and loyalty were nothing in themselves. What mattered ultimately to her was her own fortune. Her final number, the climax of the musical, was a dramatic, somewhat eerie, and finally exalting summation of her ambition and achievement. It began with strutting, brassy stripper music, continued with honky tonk, stretched dramatically into a tune of five notes repeated over and over. Merman was a mother who simply could not let go of her daughters because she dreamed for them. She faltered on the word "Momma," recovered, and faltered again, stuttered, and finally saw the plain truth. That was, as Ethan Mordden puts it, "the bitter message" the play had been shouting to Rose all along: "She can let go, perhaps, of her family, not of her obsession with stardom. Biting out a chunk of 'Everything's Coming Up Roses,' she pulls it all into a final cry for attention, *molto agitato*, . . . So, five times, she cries: 'For *me!*' "

Rightly she gives herself top billing at the end of the play, after she has sung that everything has come up roses for her. Of course, this is so because of her ferocious drive, purpose, and self-promotion. Mama Rose didn't always know best when it came to others — her precious daughters included — but she certainly knew best for herself and her own American dream.

The honesty and force of *Gypsy* accented a tragicomic story without ever diluting the musical comedy element or the sense of Americana. *Gypsy* is really a musical play with songs strategically placed to further the story and characterization. As such, it follows in the path of *Oklahoma!* (1943), and all the descendants of that

Rodgers and Hammerstein classic of American individualism. Banalities of the old musical stage — songs that could be interchanged with any number of characters, plots that made logic seem alien, dance numbers that were often defiantly gratuitous — became more intolerable after *Oklahoma!* which, as Hollis Alpert notes, "exalted the American spirit" by providing "a vision of a simpler, more golden time."

The trouble with groundbreaking in the arts is the matter of exploitation. *Oklahoma!* broke the Broadway record for long-runs (it played 2,212 performances), rewarded its investors with a 3,000 percent profit, and restored the Theatre Guild (that produced it) to fiscal health. Unfortunately, the gold mine it veined was thrown open to many vulgar exploiters who made imitation an insincere form of flattery. *Bloomer Girl* (1944), starring Celeste Holm (who had played Ado Annie in *Oklahoma!*) and with a Civil War ballet by Agnes de Mille (who had choreographed *Oklahoma!*), attempted to show the effect of war on women left behind, but the superficial and somewhat silly book undercut the attractive production. *Up in Central Park* (1945) was fustier in dialogue and prettier in its ballet, though it, too, flopped. *Blue Holiday* (1945), a Negro variety show starring Ethel Waters, the Hall Johnson Choir, and the Katherine Dunham dancers, did not survive Al Moritz's uninspiring music, and so sang the deepest blues at the box-office. Americana swelled with Gilbert and Sullivan imitations — *Memphis Bound!* (1945), a sentimental piece with a very deliberate foray into H.M.S. *Pinafore*, and *Hollywood Pinafore* (1945), with some witty though badly scattered darts from George S. Kaufman's book and lyrics, were but two examples — but the borrowings and interpolations were simply inadequate.

A partial list of the lesser-known Americana makes for humorous archival reading: *Mr. Strauss Goes to Boston* (1945), *The Girl from Nantucket* (1945), *St. Louis Woman* (1946), *Park Avenue* (1946), *Louisiana Lady* (1947), *Hold It!* (1948), *Texas, Li'l Darlin'* (1949). But Americana also had its fair share of successes after *Oklahoma!* with such shows as *Carousel* (1945), *Annie Get Your Gun* (1946), *High Button Shoes* (1947), *Kiss Me, Kate* (1948), *South Pacific* (1949), *Call Me Madam* (1950), *Guys and Dolls* (1950), *Wonderful Town* (1953), *The Pajama Game* (1954), *Damn*

Yankees (1955), *The Most Happy Fella* (1956), *Bells Are Ringing* (1956), *L'il Abner* (1956), and *The Music Man* (1957).

Carousel dispensed with the usual overture of a Broadway musical, and the picturesque New England fishing village setting provided a warm means to realizing the sentiments of a tragicomic story (adapted from Molnar's *Liliom*) of a wayward man given one precious opportunity to atone for his transgressions. There were a few critics who felt that *Carousel* was too reminiscent of *Oklahoma!* in its use of ballet to further story, but Broadway has always been very lucky in its composers and stars, and as long as there were artists such as Ethel Merman, Alfred Drake, Mary Martin, Vivian Blaine, Rosalind Russell, Gwen Verdon, Judy Holliday, Phil Silvers, and Robert Preston, and composers such as Jule Styne, Sammy Cahn, Cole Porter, Irving Berlin, Frank Loesser, Betty Comden, and Adolph Green, the musical was never in any real danger of becoming effete.

The post-war generation emerged out of economic, social, and political gloom to rediscover new wealth in America. *Annie Get Your Gun* was more of an escapist entertainment with built-in vaudevillian and Wild West set-pieces than a fully fledged musical play, but Annie Oakley was so brilliantly played by Merman for virile musical comedy as a frontier feminist ahead of her time that in addition to becoming a celebration of the Wild West and show business, the piece became a zestful comment on feminine tactics in show business, Indian affairs, and love.

High Button Shoes and *Kiss Me, Kate* dressed up conventional musical comedy in modish costumes — 1913 period ones for the former, and Elizabethan for the latter's (Shakespeare's) play-within-a(n) (American) play. The book of *High Button Shoes* was not especially witty in its adventures and misadventures of a bungling small-time con-man, but the inspired clowning of Phil Silvers and Nanette Fabray amused audiences much more than did the songs. Things were rather different in the case of *Kiss Me, Kate*. Cole Porter's superb score needed no special help from clowns, ingénues, or matinée idols, but it received, nonetheless, excellent support from the libretto of Bella and Samuel Spewack, a cast led by Alfred Drake, Patricia

Morison, and Lisa Kirk, and a romantic story of a feuding pair of actors who also happen to have once been married to each other. The triple satire (on sexual battle, Shakespeare's *The Taming of the Shrew*, and Viennese operetta) was gloriously realized, and Shakespeare became firmly memorialized in a Broadway musical.

The American heroine came to the fore in the late forties and early-to-mid fifties. Mary Martin's Nurse Nellie Forbush in *South Pacific*, Ethel Merman's Sally Adams in *Call Me Madam*, Rosalind Russell's Ruth in *Wonderful Town*, and Gwen Verdon's Lola in *Damn Yankees* — we could even add Carol Channing's Lorelei Lee in *Gentlemen Prefer Blondes* (1949) — were all fascinating parts of a flamboyant kaleidoscope, in which the American heroine was mythicized. Trouble was that none of these women had the stage quite to herself, except at select moments when she had a sparkling turn. Arkansan Nellie Forbush has a radiant good nature, and Mary Martin's straightforward, buoyant warmth was perfect for her, but it is Emile DeBecque who has the best romantic song ("Some Enchanted Evening"), and the plot is a compression of short stories from James A. Michener. Ethel Merman certainly had a vehicle as Sally Adams, Ambassador to fictional Lichtenburg (modelled after Pearl Mesta, Washington heiress and Truman's minister to Luxembourg), but *Call Me Madam* was what Gerald Bordman in *American Musical Theatre: A Chronicle* calls "a reversion to the topical musicals of the thirties" and so had nothing to live after its dated satire, apart from "You're Just in Love" — a song that received four or five encores a night and then turned into a pop hit by Bing Crosby's recording.

Carol Channing, too, had a star vehicle in an otherwise period-piece — this one about the roaring twenties in which crafty Lorelei shone out like the diamonds she so cleverly appropriated as her best friends. A musical version of Anita Loos's best-selling novel of more than two decades earlier, this show made a cult figure out of a shrewdly manipulative heroine from Little Rock who used vulnerability and innocence as a mask for her acquisitiveness. With a voice that modulated swiftly from a babyish squeal to a baritone growl, Channing made the part her own. Nostalgia, once again, was strong, and this musical revived the sort of lightweight pleasures that had been rampant in the era of *No, No, Nanette* (1925) and her immediate successors.

Wonderful Town was clever and knowing, a technical *tour de force* (in script and music) as a musical rendition of Joseph Fields and Jerome Chodorov's *My Sister Eileen*, and Rosalind Russell, who had first played Ruth in the movie version of the straight play, found a musical role she could inhabit with her inimitable confidence, grace, and exuberance, though her limitations as a singer and dancer could not be camouflaged. Neither could anyone hide the fact that this musical play was more of a nostalgia piece than a transcendant opus — a sort of homage to sisterly feeling and a vanished urban innocence. It was a folk tale with a sophisticated score (by Leonard Bernstein), a good script, and strong performances by Russell and Edie Adams as the demure, coquettish title-character.

Americana was also deftly served by *Guys and Dolls* and *The Pajama Game*, though in the first instance, the Damon Runyon source (with its Bronx argot and tough underworld caricatures) touched up the story with folk exotica. The central plot involving the unusual romance between Sky Masterson, a professional gambler, and Sister Sarah Brown, a Salvation Army worker, was itself exotic for being so incongruous. And the mixture of hardboiled and sentimental characters, given their symphony of flashy, ungrammatical patter, made for a raffish atmosphere that was colourful, loud, and highly entertaining. Loesser's clever and catchy songs, Jo Mielziner's highly unusual set designs (especially the underground tunnel used for the "floating crap game"), and the impeccable ensemble work made for a musical comedy masterpiece.

Equally native in grain and texture, *The Pajama Game*, adapted from Richard Bissell's novel, *7½ Cents*, was a noisy, coarse, somewhat socialist musical satire that glorified unionism and attacked Big Business. Directed by George Abbott and Jerome Robbins, and choreographed by Bob Fosse (with Robbins), it might not have triumphed without the fast, funny dances (particularly Carol Haney's "Steam Heat" number with Buzz Miller and Peter Gennaro) and the directorial inventiveness which lifted the production above pedestrian situations and a most unpromising basis for a musical. The sparkling pace and Fosse's jazzy, offbeat dances, replete with signature snapping fingers and pelvic posturings, captivated audiences who might have initially had severe misgivings about attending a musical based on management-employee relationships in a garment factory. When *My Fair Lady* graced the Broadway scene in 1956, charming audiences with its literate grace and comic romanticism, standards for musical comedy rose particularly high. For once, the book was given its proper due as a basis for civilized entertainment, and all the noisy muscle-flexing in comic caperings and musical exuberance of earlier musicals seemed light and superficial in the face of a well-made story with serious themes, witty dialogue, and characters resonant with reality. Not that *My Fair Lady* was the first genuine musical play with serious subjects. Rodgers and Hammerstein, Kurt Weill, Frank Loesser, and Arthur Laurents had all turned out dramatic texts, where realism and sometimes even tragedy dominated a world previously congenial only to escapism. *Show Boat* (1927), *Porgy and Bess* (1935), *Johnny Johnson* (1936), *Knickerbocker Holiday* (1938), and *Lady in the Dark* (1941) also dealt with profound subjects, but these were either operettas or operas, and several had enough left-wing or ultra-liberal propaganda to put off many audiences. Besides, only Moss Hart's *Lady in the Dark*, with a score by Kurt Weill and lyrics by Ira Gershwin, qualified as a musical comedy, though its dream obsession and elegant dialogue left little impression on the Broadway scene.

The real American comic masterworks — that is, musical comedies with American characters and American backgrounds, with identifiable American preoccupations — occurred in the latter-half of the fifties, though not before some very mixed offerings. *Plain and Fancy* (1955) was perhaps too novel and particular, for in avoiding all the easy theatrical tricks — except for a ballet — it made its audiences concentrate their sympathies on a stern Amish philosophy and a frequently difficult way of life. *Damn Yankees*, as Gerald Bordman contends, "hit a metaphoric grand slam." The Faustian legend cast in a baseball setting was a case of deliberately Americanizing a myth, and the show wickedly played off the nation's chagrin at the baseball omnipotence of the New York Yankees. Critics did not agree on the quality of Frank Loesser's *The Most Happy Fella* (1956) — an adaptation of Sidney Howard's hit of the 1924-25 season, *They Knew What They Wanted* — and its often maudlin sentimentality was a drawback, though this was countered by some operatic songs and a three-act structure — rare in modern musicals. *L'il Abner* was a cornpone aberration — a Dogpatch musical aimed at a less intellectual crowd — which it certainly found for just under 700 performances. Higher up in scale, intelligence, and achievement was Comden and Green's *Bells Are Ringing*, a conventional musical perfectly aware of its own modest ambition and lack of pretension. Jule Styne's score was "comfortably old hat," the plot involving a romance between an eavesdropping telephone-operator and an aspiring playwright was comfortably mediocre, but the performance of Judy Holliday was inspired and barmy. Walter Kerr found the production "homey, comfortable," while Richard Watts, Jr. praised its "warm-hearted friendliness" that was "wonderfully endearing."

There seemed to be an overriding need among audiences for shows that put a bloom on things. Meredith Wilson's *The Music Man* (1957) was a benevolently optimistic version of 1912 America, and its glib rogue-hero, Harold Hill, underwent a very moral transformation all in the cause of love and family values. The show's appeal lay in its rich local colour, its likeable characters — including the con artist Harold Hill — and its charm. There were softshoe routines and barbershop quartet songs to balance against the noisy trombone march, and, as Hollis Alpert notes, Raoul Pène du Bois's costumes in "shades of vanilla fudge ice cream and raspberry sundaes" added to the beaming good nature of the show. It was all innocent and very Fourth of July, and in retrospect it was a perfect musical for inveterate Republicans, none of whom would ever be troubled by its ambivalences.

Rodgers and Hammerstein's *Flower Drum Song* (1958), graced with enough Oriental elements to revive memories of *The King and I* (1951), was lavish in its production values but too exclusive in its San Francisco Chinatown setting and Chinese-American characters to be truly rooted in the American grain, and its contrived sentimentality marred the libretto.

19

Which brings us back to *Gypsy* (1959) — not, perhaps, a pure musical comedy (given its plot about a misguided mother and her miscalculated dreams) but a wonderfully structured play, strong with both implicit and explicit comedy, always on the mark about the absurdities of show business and its obsessive dreamers. When *Gypsy* barged its way onto Broadway, it found itself alone in its risk with a benevolent monster, Mama Rose — a sort of backstage Mother Courage who learns that she must live her own and not her children's lives. Alpert observes that it had a taut, lean, pungent libretto where "almost every one of the scenes ended with a song and a blackout, to be immediately followed, seamlessly, by the next scene." Though Ethel Merman made it her own show by her bravura performance, *Gypsy* was a marvel in its own right: what Bordman calls a musical "filled with all the old musical comedy tricks: burlesque routines, strip-teases, soft-shoe dances, rousing choruses, and love songs"; a relentless chronicle in which all the lyrics, stemming from character and situation, "propelled the action and deepened the characterizations." In short, it was what we would call an integrated musical comedy — a true American phenomenon that was also a connoisseur's dream.

A Hard-Boiled Rose

THE MUSICAL'S TITLE is a little trick of sorts, for *Gypsy* refers, of course, to Gypsy Rose Lee, the acknowledged Queen of Burlesque, while also connecting with other "gypsies" — the dancers and performers who wander from town to town, circuit to circuit, living out of suitcases in a quest for the Big Break. In her colourful memoir, the legendary Gypsy (born Rose Louise Hovick) recounts how and why she changed her name as she watched a worker put up the marquee for her first lead billing. The words "Rose Louise" would reveal to everyone in the family and close friends that she was now a burlesque performer: "Everyone would know — June and Gordon and Stanley and Grandpa — Grandpa! Suddenly all the joy was out of it. Grandpa wouldn't like it at all. He didn't even approve of the Pantages Circuit." So she quickly changed her name to "Rose Lee" and then just as quickly added "Gypsy" to it on a whim.

But the trick up the musical's sleeve is the "gypsy" mother behind Rose Louise — the itinerant concocter of novelty acts for her two daughters and the unapologetically eccentric and relentlessly scheming pursuer of a Show Biz dream. It isn't simply playwright Arthur Laurents who has Mama Rose steal the spotlight; in her memoir, Gypsy Rose Lee herself gives front and centre to her mother. After all, Mama Rose has the surprises, the outrageous stratagems, the undaunted chutzpah, the irresistible punch-lines, the sheer feverous bravado to function purposefully amid chaos and dream a dream for her children and herself. America has always loved the valiant underdog, and Mama Rose (in her elder daughter's memoir and in the musical) refuses to be discouraged even when the real sky seems ready to fall on her domain of make-believe. It is Mama Rose who wants to read fortunes like a gypsy — her daughters' and her own

— but only as long as she can invent a gloriously happy ending. It is she who looks on The Road as her personal odyssey for good fortune and happiness. And it is she who always manages to be exotic and, therefore, somewhat disconcerting to those who cannot understand or appreciate her sense of idiosyncratic adventure. It is she who carries the girls' music, draws up the contracts, and barges down a dark aisle of the theatre, crying out advice to her performing daughters. Like a gypsy, she can dissemble (feigning severe personal injury at times to elicit sympathy and a tidy bit of pecuniary compensation) and steal (anything from hotel blankets to props from a burlesque joint). And like a gypsy, she thrives on fabrication and fantasy. Even as she bustles her young daughters along a frequently tawdry theatre circuit, she sees the world of tinsel unreality as a magical place, glorying in the music, lights, and applause.

She is a character who, if herself a little fabricated in the memoir, is compellingly real to us. Reading about her life where one outrageous and wonderful thing follows another, we don't mind if some of it is an invention for readers. Her character and her life are a performance — a piquant series of turns or set-pieces, amid which she espouses a belief in divine protection while carrying a heavy club just in case!

Mama's genealogy has a touch of the legendary about it, even though her parents are from Seattle. Her own mother was a tall, elegant hatmaker, fondly and perhaps a little fearfully nicknamed "Big Lady." She travelled a great deal, although forbidden to do so by her husband. He did not approve of Big Lady's jaunts, but there wasn't much he could do about them. Gypsy remembers how "she would pack a trunk with expensive-looking hats and travel to Juneau, or Tonopah or any place where ladies went who could afford the elaborate hats Big Lady made and who were flashy enough to appreciate them." Mama Rose evidently inherited some of this fearlessness and urge to wander in pursuit of financial advancement. Lucky she was to have a precocious performer in Baby June, a "Pocketsized Pavlova," a toe-tapping tot. Because the elder girl, Rose Louise, couldn't sing and was overweight, she was pushed into the chorus, before being allowed to sing "I'm a Hard-boiled Rose."

Mama (both inadvertently and deliberately) never kept correct track of her daughters' ages, which was particularly to her advantage when questioned by policemen who were eager to prove child exploitation. As Gypsy wrote: "On trains June was under five, I was under ten. In Syracuse we both had to be twelve. We couldn't play New York City at all, because the age limit there was sixteen, and even with lifts in our shoes we couldn't look sixteen." Mama's courage (and Baby June's talent) carried the vaudeville act for several years, and when Dainty June (as she became known as a teenager) eloped with an older boy, it was Mama's ferocious ambition, indomitable will, and inviolable audacity that carried her quest farther.

Eccentric in the pets she kept (Gussie the temperamental goose, Gigolo the monkey, Waupie the incontinent lamb, plus a number of dogs) and eccentric in her dress (a bouclé suit and fur cape cut down from an old beaver coat, and an oversized floppy bow in her hair), she would stalk the Keith-Orpheum circuit like "a jungle mother, and she knew too well that in a jungle it doesn't pay to be nice." She would steal ideas from other shows or acts without any acknowledgement as such, and her own highly idiosyncratic sense of morality permitted only self-justification:

In her more dramatic moods she would add, "I'm a woman alone in the world with two babies to support." She said this years after June and I were out of the baby stage, and even after there were three ex-husbands contributing to our support, but that was a detail Mother always chose to forget until the alimony checks were past due. Mother didn't call it alimony. If it was mentioned at all, it was "a financial settlement."

Her daughter June Havoc wrote that Rose's dishonesty "was utterly honest; her logic was invincible. Besides, she always had some impressive axiom at hand to shore up her statements, such as, 'Keep smiling, all the world loves a laugher.' Or 'It's a long road that has no detours.' "

Mama was born to be theatrical. June believed that Rose would have been a great actress because she had all the requirements: "Her

23

imagination was so powerful that once she said a thing she wanted to be true, or wished had happened, it became a reality to her. She really believed that, having uttered the words, they would be accepted as fact. She was convincing at all times." She would wring every stranger's tear-ducts by playing the role of a mother bravely protecting her two "babies" against an uncaring world. When frightened or angry, she would suffer (or feign) asthmatic attacks, but it wasn't often that she could be frightened, for she took on any adversity and any man with the resourcefulness of a born heroine. And always with an eye for effect. When she engaged a private tutor for her daughters, she insisted that Miss Tompkins, a blue-eyed, full-figure blonde, wear her hair straight, a black dress with white piqué collar and cuffs, sturdy "ground grippers," and horn-rimmed glasses. "Not real lenses, of course," Gypsy said gaily. "Just glass in the horn rims for effect."

For Dainty June's finale, Mama Rose dressed her in a gown entirely covered with rhinestones, and concocted a program note to state that the dress cost $1000 and had a million stones on the skirts alone. She had to be dissuaded from adding that three women had gone blind working on it.

Pretence was the essence of Mama Rose's mode and, perhaps, her ultimate fatal flaw as a mother and person. Her younger daughter was more mordant than Gypsy in seeing through her ruses and pretenses. While recognizing the family trait of wanting "everything that being alive suggested," June Havoc blamed Rose for wanting to keep her perpetually a child and for being a wedge between her and sister Gypsy. Mama Rose would pretend about life even as she lay dying from cancer in 1954. June had become a successful Broadway performer and movie actress in her own right, but she was never allowed to forget that she had "abandoned" her mother and sister and thrown away her chance for fame in vaudeville and burlesque. And even though Gypsy had been the consort of several leading showmen (including Billy Rose, Mike Todd, and Otto Preminger) and had won effusive tributes from artists as diverse as John Steinbeck, S.J. Perelman, and Tennessee Williams, she was never allowed to forget Mama Rose's role in her own legend. Before breathing her last on her deathbed, Mama had strong parting words to the daughters:

"This isn't the end. Wherever you go, as long as either of you lives, I'll be right there — and I swear before God you're always going to know it! . . . You'll know I'm there, I'll see to that. So go on, Louise, tell all your classy friends how funny I was, how much smarter you were than me. When you get your own private kick in the ass, just remember: it's a present from me to you. A present from your funny, unbright mother."

Talk about a curtain line! Could a playwright do better? It appears from the available evidence and especially from Gypsy Rose Lee's memoir (which is divided into three acts just like a play) that her life disposed itself to drama and comedy. Mama Rose always pretended that it had been a Cinderella story, particularly for Gypsy. The finale of Act III in the memoir seals this theme: "I closed my eyes and along with the familiar noise of the train Mother seemed to be telling me again how lucky I was. 'What a wonderful life you've had — the music, lights, applause — everything in the world a girl could ask for. . . .'"

The real question is whether this was a Cinderella story in which Mama Rose was the Cinderella who always managed to postpone the dreaded stroke of midnight and who never really cared about a Prince Charming. In short, the question is whether Mama Rose lived her own fable more for herself than for her daughters and whether she was a sane or demented heroine.

This question did not, of course, suggest itself to Gypsy Rose Lee who began the actual writing of her memoir in February 1956, during a four-week layoff between the closing of *Twentieth Century* at the Palm Beach Playhouse and the opening of her act at the Sans Souci Hotel in Miami Beach. Her son, Erik Lee Preminger, who was entertained throughout his boyhood by the anecdotes and stories of her childhood, describes her as being an inveterate tale-spinner — a woman with a gift for relating the most colourful, exciting vignettes so spellbindingly that he would hang upon every word even though he had heard the same stories over and over, though with curious changes from version to version. But she was never much bothered by historical inaccuracy: it was less important to her than a good punch line. Like her mother, she was best when inventing on the spur of the moment — like the time she drew columnist Leonard Lyons's attention at Sardi's by promising him a "very funny story" which, she admits, didn't as yet exist, and which she had to fabricate on the spur of the moment. A sort of Auntie Mame of burlesque, she conquered men and life by her spirit and humour. She emphasized "tease" over "strip," remaining covered for almost the entire act. And her lyrics — which she apparently created herself — were witty enough to amuse sophisticates such as Anita Loos, Cholly Knickerbocker, Gertrude Lawrence, and O.O. McIntyre (who described her as having "a cough drop voice and a dress suit accent" with which to scatter French phrases). A brief quotation, from Erik Lee Preminger's *Gypsy & Me*, should suggest the flavour of her stage persona:

> When I raise my skirts with slyness and dexterity,
> I'm mentally computing just how much I'll give to charity.
>
> And though my thighs I have revealed,
> And just a bit of me remains concealed,
> I'm thinking of the life of Duse.
> Or the third chapter of the *Rise and Fall of the Roman Empire*.

Given her lack of formal education, the facility with long rhymes, the amusingly ironic allusions, the sheer masquerade of affectation are all surprisingly keen. She is said to have credited George Davis (an important figure on the New York literary scene) with getting her started as a writer. Described by Janet Flanner as being "a sulky, ultrasensitive, brilliant character and a deadly wit" (quoted in the afterword of Lee's memoir), he became fiction editor of *Harper's Bazaar*, where he introduced readers to serious fiction and helped promote the talents of Carson McCullers and Truman Capote. In the 1940s his Manhattan apartment attracted as boarders W.H. Auden, Benjamin Britten, Oliver Smith, Paul and Jane Bowles, and

Gypsy Rose Lee, who wrote over a dozen articles and her first book, *The G-String Murders*, while living there. As a headline-grabbing star, she rode in a chauffeured maroon and gray Rolls Royce with her initials in gold on the door, but she was equally at home with a hot-plate. As one who had worked with Fanny Brice, Bobby Clark, Jimmy Durante, Randolph Scott, Christopher Plummer, and Ethel Merman, she was a woman with a mind who could match wits with such comics as Imogene Coca, Hermione Gingold, and Nancy Walker. When she decided that she was too old to take off her clothes in public, she feared the future. Having been nurtured and pampered by her twenty-six year career, she did not have another viable means of support or ego-stroking. Preminger notes that "everything else she had done since 1930 — Broadway, films, mystery novels, even a radio show — had been marginally successful at best, and that had derived primarily from the novelty value of a stripper working in her clothes instead of out of them." A middle-aged woman, without a career and with enormous expenses, she felt she was in an unenviable position.

She turned to writing to resolve the problem. She rented a type-writer, checked herself and son Erik into a cheap efficiency motel and stuck to an unvarying routine for the entire month. Her son recounts how she'd get them both up "at the shriek of dawn" for breakfast. Then she would send him off with his lunch to spend the day at the local fishing pier while she worked. "Late in the afternoon I'd come home, she'd let me read her day's output and we'd discuss it while she made dinner, then we'd watch a little TV and go to bed."

She devoted herself to the book "with the kind of obsessive intensity that marked everything that she did." She called her work area in her bedroom the "snake pit," and except for a one-week interruption to do the "U.S. Steel Hour" on television and a five-week summer stock tour with *Fancy Meeting You Again*, she sustained this schedule until the completion of her book on December 26. "She used to say," said her son, that "*Gypsy* took her nine months and was a much more difficult pregnancy than having me."

The memoir is an entrancing read, with one outrageous and wonderful incident following hard upon another. Act I spans the childhood years of the Hovick sisters, and although it is filled with memories of the Keith-Orpheum and Minsky circuits, it darkens with a potentially tragic element, when June elopes with her lover, causing Mama Rose to feel betrayed, angry, yet determined. Act II takes us back to where Act I had begun — Seattle and Rose's home — but it isn't long before the chronicle of tours and gigs recommences. Comic characters and incidents crowd the pages, as Gypsy begins her ascent to Ziegfeld's Follies and an acquaintanceship with gangster Waxy Gordon. Act III marks the end of an era, but Mama Rose won't have it as such. She holds firm to her notion of a Cinderella story, and she is given the final say. Although meant to be Gypsy's autobiography, it is really Rose's book — simply because she makes her presence felt throughout. It is her quips and deceits that we remember best. It is she with the vivid personality that stays in the mind. June is mostly experienced as an absent figure. Gypsy is pulled offstage, as it were, by her backstage mother.

Gypsy was accepted by Harper and Brothers, who were convinced that it would be a major best-seller. They rushed it into production. But she was more cautious for she recalled that her second novel, *Mother Finds a Body*, flopped badly after the success of her first, *The G-String Murders*. Determined to avoid a repetition of that failure, she laboured for eighteen hours a day on the book's release. She corrected galleys, selected photographs, and prepared excerpts for magazines, but she spent most of her time orchestrating a publicity campaign. Publicity was free and her forté. As an unknown stripper newly arrived in New York in 1932, she knew how to command free press. She would flatter influential columnists with sweet notes and pleasantries until they gave in to her sycophancy with gushing tributes in their papers. This talent for working her name into the social and entertainment news was combined with a daring business sense. Between costume fittings for a movie role in *Wind across the Everglades*, written by Budd Schulberg and directed by Nicholas Ray, she was in meetings with her lawyers to decide on bids for dramatic rights to *Gypsy*.

The critics had liked *Gypsy*, which was reprinted in England and Italy, with excerpts appearing in *Harper's* and *Town & Country*. The book even made the New York Times best-seller list, and MGM and Warner Brothers were each offering about $200,000 for film rights, while David Merrick and the team of Lerner and Loewe were bidding for Broadway musical rights. Surprisingly, she sold the rights to Merrick for $4,000 and a percentage of the box-office gross. "You turned down two hundred thousand dollars?" asked her son incredulously:

"It's a risk," she explained, "but if the show is successful I'll get royalties from it for the rest of my life as well as at least that much when it's sold for a film."

"But why David Merrick instead of Lerner and Loewe?" [She liked him, she replied, because he was young and aggressive and reminded her a lot of Mike Todd whom she had loved and once sponsored financially.]

Shrewdness informed her daring, and both were qualities that attracted strong men to her. She had once played Barnum to Todd, becoming his partner for Star and Garter (1942), a high-class burlesque ("tall dames and low comedy," quips Todd) and both had gotten rich in the process. It became the showman's longest-running Broadway show and his second biggest money-maker. The Lee-Todd business relationship, however, quickly sagged with The Naked Genius, Lee's first play, which Todd produced and which starred Joan Blondell, the saucy Warner Brothers musical girl who was to become his next wife. The fundamental trouble was the script, which was about a famous stripteaser, Honey Bee Carroll, who writes a book in order to enhance her image. In the course of this endeavour, she falls in love with the publisher's son, but decides, just before the wedding and the final curtain, that her heart belongs to show business and her manager. Much of this material was autobiographical, but the plot was farfetched and corny. After daily revisions, Gypsy asked that her credit be changed to read, "Written by Louise Hovick." "And Mr. Todd," piped up George S. Kaufman, the director, "change my credit to: 'Directed by Jed Harris.' " One New York paper called the show "a dreary witless mess." The New York Times simply advised (with a pun probably intended): "Mr Todd: Take It Off." Yet the show made money. So Gypsy Rose Lee survived the disaster and Todd's passion for Joan Blondell with over a hundred thousand dollars added to her bank account. She didn't win Todd as a husband, but she increased her finances.

Having sung for so many years about being "a hard-boiled Rose," she proved to have actually become one.

Laurents's Book

DAVID MERRICK (born David Margulois, 1911, in St. Louis) was an experienced lawyer who had served under Herman Shumlin before branching out as Broadway producer. His first success was *Fanny* (1954), but others quickly followed: *The Matchmaker* (1955), *Look Back in Anger* (1957), *The Entertainer* (1958), and *La Plume de Ma Tante* (1958). An eclectic list, to say the least, spanning the gamut of authors from Marcel Pagnol and Thornton Wilder to John Osborne and Robert Dhéry, and performers from Ruth Gordon and Laurence Olivier to Kenneth Haigh and Brenda de Banzie. Merrick gambled with his enterprises, with no guarantees that Broadway audiences would take to French provincialism, a British angry young playwright, or old-fashioned American farce. But Merrick was a keen gambler and a master of publicity. Who but he would have hired a woman to climb on stage and slap the actor portraying Jimmy Porter in *Look Back in Anger*? Merrick was nobody's fool. He had an eye for artistic possibility as much as he had a yen for making money. Theatre scholar Stanley Green recounts how Merrick immediately saw the musical possibilities in *Gypsy*, the memoir, when he read only a chapter from it in *Harper's Magazine* in 1957. Without even bothering to read the entire book, he placed himself in the bidding for rights and won.

His co-producer was Leland Hayward, a former scenarist and Hollywood producer who had also been a successful agent for such clients as James Stewart, Frederic March, Henry Fonda, Charles Laughton, Ginger Rogers, Greta Garbo, Myrna Loy, Ben Hecht, Edna Ferber, Ernest Hemingway, et cetera. Hayward's production credits were impressive — both on stage and screen. In Hollywood he had made *The Spirit of St. Louis* with James Stewart, *Mister Roberts* with Henry Fonda repeating his Broadway role, and *The Old Man and the Sea* with Spencer Tracy. His career as Broadway producer had begun in 1944 with *A Bell for Adano*, starring Frederic March. This was followed by *State of the Union* (1945), which won the Pulitzer Prize for its authors Howard Lindsay and Russel Crouse, the Tony-winning *Mister Roberts* (1947), *Anne of The Thousand Days* (1948) with Rex Harrison, *South Pacific* (1949) with Mary Martin, *The Wisteria Trees* (1950) with Helen Hayes, *Daphne Laureola* (1950) with Edith Evans, and *Call Me Madam* (1950) with Merman. The three diverse productions in the same year all showed the risks that Hayward was prepared to take and his dedication to quality, regardless of the source or nature of a script. *Gypsy* was to be his sixteenth stage production.

Merrick recruited Jule Styne, Betty Comden, and her partner, Adolph Green to work out a libretto. Gypsy Rose Lee's memoir had the potential of being turned into a radically different musical. Theodore Taylor observes that while it had opportunities for big onstage numbers, it seemed to lend itself better to being adapted into "a straight play with an overlay of music and dance." But Styne and his collaborators found that the characters of Rose and Baby June posed real problems of focus and presentation. "Okay, if you don't like it," said Styne one day, "let's tell Merrick we don't do it." But Comden and Green weren't prepared to do that yet. When in the spring they accepted an offer from Warner Brothers to write the screenplay for *Auntie Mame*, they promised Merrick that they would not neglect their work on *Gypsy*. Styne, however, felt that the duo was not fully committed any longer to the project: "Obviously, they'd cooled on it. So did I, at that time. I'd worked with them long enough to know that if they really felt strongly about something they'd move along with it."

Finally, in late August, Comden and Green returned their advance to Merrick because, as Craig Zadan says, "they just couldn't figure out a way of doing it." Styne, for his part, had already begun work on *Say, Darling* (1958), a bizarre musical that was what Bordman calls "a play based on a book about making a musical out of another book." The book in question was a novel by Richard Bissell that recounted the production difficulties of turning his earlier work,

7 ½ Cents, into *The Pajama Game*. Despite an amusing performance by Robert Morse as an eager young producer, and a year's run, the show was not considered a critical success.

In the early summer of 1958, Styne heard that *Gypsy* was "on" again. What he did not know at the time was that Arthur Laurents, who eventually produced the libretto, had not been approached directly by David Merrick. It was Merrick's co-producer, Leland Hayward, who called Laurents to say that Jerome Robbins would direct the show if Laurents wrote the book. This was ironic, for Robbins and Laurents were not on very good terms as a result of Robbins's behaviour on *West Side Story*. Still, Laurents (in his own words) "wasn't going to allow personal problems to get in the way of a good project and, still, no one can stage a number better than Jerry."

Laurents was a reputable playwright, born in the Bronx (July 14, 1918), reared in the Flatbush section of Brooklyn, who had majored in English at Cornell University, and moved on to television, Broadway, and films after experiences in night-club revues and radio plays. During his enlistment years in a paratroop unit at Fort Benning, Georgia, he had worked on military training films, while also writing scripts for radio programs designed to educate the public about the problems of returning servicemen. *Assignment Home* won a Variety Poll Radio Award as one of the outstanding shows of 1945. Another script, *About Face*, was included in *The Best One-Act Plays of 1945–46*. After doing research for *Assignment Home*, Laurents was inspired to write his searing psychological drama about a battle-scarred Jewish ex-soldier who faces anti-Semitism. *Home of the Brave* opened to mixed reviews at the Belasco Theatre on Broadway in December 1945, and even though it closed after only sixty-nine performances, many critics acknowledged it to be a significant contribution to postwar American theatre. Alas, the film version directed by Carl Foreman, which followed in 1949, turned the role of the Jew into a black man because Jews "had been done" in such movies as *Gentleman's Agreement*. Laurents, who had already failed with a second Broadway play in 1947, was angry but persevered in a Hollywood career. He did the screenplays for *Rope* (1948), *The Snake Pit* (1948), and *Anna Lucasta* (1949).

Broadway and Hollywood shared his attention. After failing on stage with *The Bird Cage* (1950), a melodrama about the backstage troubles of a ruthlessly tyrannical cabaret owner, Laurents came up with a charming winner in *The Time of the Cuckoo* (1952), a rueful comedy about a lonely American spinster (played by Shirley Booth) who finds brief romance with a married Italian shopkeeper during a summer holiday in Venice. This hit won a Tony for Booth and was later filmed by David Lean as a vehicle for Katharine Hepburn, although with a new title, *Summertime* (1955).

Another Broadway play came between film scripts for Anatole Litvak's *Anastasia* (1956), starring Ingrid Bergman, and Otto Preminger's *Bonjour Tristesse* (1958), starring Jean Seberg. However, yet again, Laurents discovered that any previous Broadway success was no guarantee of continuing critical favour. *A Clearing in the Woods* (1957), with Kim Stanley as a neurotic woman who confronts her past selves (played by three different actresses), was ambitious but laboured. It had only a three-and-a-half week run. Yet Laurents persisted as a playwright, for he disliked the crass commercialism of Hollywood and the studios' tendency to dehumanize the profession. In theatre he felt in contact with people; in Hollywood studios he heard only a clock, a cash register, and the anxieties of producers who wanted a product as quickly and as cheaply as possible. Broadway rewarded him with his biggest stage success yet, when *West Side Story* premièred in 1957. Although the critical reception was mixed — with most critics considering the libretto far inferior to Shakespeare's *Romeo and Juliet*, to which it bore many contemporary correspondences — the show was recognized as a bold new kind of musical theatre which carried the American musical idiom far away from Kern, Gershwin, Rodgers and Hammerstein. In truth, most of the plaudits went to Jerome Robbins's choreography and Leonard Bernstein's score, and the musical gained in stature only after the film version in 1961.

When Hayward offered him the commission to adapt *Gypsy*, Laurents quickly read Gypsy Rose Lee's memoir and thought it "fun, jazzy." But he wasn't interested in the "strip-tease queen of America," says Zadan, and didn't think anybody else would be either, so he declined. "I read the book and I thought that it was kind of jazzy, but I didn't see where I came in." Hayward, who never took "no" for an answer, persisted in his pleading and assured him that he would find some way to interest the public in *Gypsy*. Then one day, several guests visited Laurents's beach-home for drinks, and in the course of this visit, one young woman spoke about Gypsy Rose Lee's mother who apparently was a curvaceous, plump blonde — "sort of like Shirley Booth. . . . Very sweet and an absolute killer."

According to Zadan, Laurents was fascinated by this gossip. He reconsidered and had the idea of "parents who live their children's lives." Laurents returned to Hayward and Merrick and announced that if he could figure out a way that the star could top the strip number in the end, then he would do the show. Laurents realized that Louise was going to have to turn into a strip queen, but this development could not be the climax because the story was really about the mother. Taylor states that he then "got the idea for 'Rose's Turn,' in which that overwhelming need for recognition came out, after which the whole piece fell into place." Says Zadan: "Robbins had conceived 'Rose's Turn' as a ballet in which all of the characters would appear. Unable to make the dance work, he finally asked that the number be done as a solo song instead."

Laurents stipulated that he wanted to approach Ethel Merman himself in order to lure her to the starring role. He didn't need any special strategy, however, to get Merman who, while at a cocktail party in Gypsy Rose Lee's elegant Manhattan townhouse, announced to her hostess: "I've read your book. I love it. I want to do it. I'm going to do it. And I'll shoot anyone else who gets the part."

Laurents had never met Merman, but was certainly one of her musical comedy fans. He took her to Sardi's, where she had a Horse's Neck. Their conversation, as recorded in Merman's autobiography, went something like this:

"I want to do a show, but I don't want to do the usual Ethel Merman musical."

"Neither do I," retorted the actress.

"This woman is a monster. How far are you willing to go?"

"As far as you want me to. . . . Nobody's ever given me the chance before."

So it was obvious from the outset that the show needed a Merman, but no more than she needed it.

Merman already had a considerable Broadway reputation, based chiefly on her iron-lungs, impeccable comic timing, and verve with playing tough and brassy, funny and sassy roles. Born Ethel Zimmerman in Astoria, Queens, and once a secretary for a vacuum booster brake firm, Merman (her stage name the result of surgery on her family name) became the favourite singer of the Gershwins, Irving Berlin, and Cole Porter. While working as a stenographer-typist, she did nightclub appearances at such venues as Keen's English Chop House and Little Russia, where she came to the attention of Lou Irwin, theatrical agent for Helen Morgan, the Ritz Brothers, Brian Aherne, and others. A career in musical short subjects at Warner Brothers quickly followed, though she never really caught on in films. Fortunately, Broadway realized her value and took her to its bosom. She had an unbroken string of hits: *Girl Crazy* (1930), *George White's Scandals* (Eleventh Edition) (1931), *Humpty Dumpty* (1932), *Take a Chance* (1932), *Anything Goes* (1934), *Red, Hot and Blue* (1936), *Stars in Your Eyes* (1939), *Du Barry Was a Lady* (1939), *Panama Hattie* (1940), *Something for the Boys* (1943), *Annie Get Your Gun* (1946), *Call Me Madam* (1950), and *Happy Hunting* (1956). None of these ran less than six months. She was lucky enough to have had the songs in her first show written by George and Ira Gershwin. Cole Porter had composed the songs for five other of her shows; Irving Berlin for two of her greatest. Berlin once warned: "You'd better not write a bad lyric for Merman because people will hear it in the second balcony."

And Porter, who once said that she sounded like a band going by, paid her her favourite compliment: "I'd rather write songs for Ethel Merman than anyone else in the world," perhaps because she never changed a word or tampered with the melodies or rhythms. Toscanini once remarked that she was like another instrument in the band — in other words, loud but honest.

And it wasn't just her belting voice and delivery that drew praise.

Bertolt Brecht admired her and so did his widow, Helene Weigel, who wanted Merman to play the title role in *Mother Courage* in New York. In fact, Weigel, a legendary Mother Courage with the Berliner Ensemble, once remarked that Merman was the only actress who influenced her performance. "In the scene where Mother Courage refused to identify her dead son, Madame Weigel said she allowed her jaw to drop in silent horror" — the sort of pantomime used by Merman, along with shrunken shoulders, legs wide open at the knees, and a caved-in diaphragm — to achieve a "goon" effect when she fell in love with Frank Butler in *Annie Get Your Gun*.

Actually, although *Annie* was a high point in her career, it was simply a culmination of singing and comic effects she had long mastered. Cole Porter, who had analyzed her voice and turned out songs to show off its variety, gave her a new kind of love song to make her very own in *Anything Goes*. "You're the Top" and "I Get a Kick out of You" were the biggest hits of that show, especially when she broke a single word, such as "terrifically," into syllables and held the second syllable daringly. But a close competitor was "Blow, Gabriel, Blow," a loud pseudo-spiritual, that allowed her to pull out all the stops. In *Du Barry Was a Lady*, she proved that she could match physical gags with Bert Lahr — which did nothing, alas, to cure Lahr's chronic insecurity. She showed that she was no hit-or-miss comedienne but an expert technician who could go through her paces show after show without losing crispness or timing. After watching nightly for a couple of weeks, the librettist Buddy De Sylva commented: "Watching Merman is like watching a motion picture. . . . Her performance never varies." This was meant as a compliment, and it established what was becoming crystal-clear: she could carry a show. The Merman cachet for brassy broads was honed in *Panama Hattie*, where the title-character was quite a dame who socialized with sailors and didn't speak with correct gentility, but who had a soft side.

But *Annie Get Your Gun* gave her two extra fillips as a Broadway star: a great entrance and the best musical score she had yet enjoyed. Annie Oakley was a fully fledged woman who sang everything from risqué comic songs to sentimental ballads. Her share included "Doin'

What Comes Natur'lly," "You Can't Get a Man with a Gun," "There's No Business Like Show Business," "They Say It's Wonderful," "Moonshine Lullaby,' "I'm an Indian Too," "I Got Lost in His Arms," "I Got the Sun in the Morning," and "Anything You Can Do, I Can Do Better." There were enough signature songs to last an entire career, if necessary, but for Merman there were more to come with *Call Me Madam*, where she played a version of Pearl Mesta, American Ambassador Extraordinary and Plenipotentiary to Luxembourg — though the truth is that she was bigger and better than her songs.

Then there was a three-year absence from Broadway, after professional unpleasantries with co-stars in *Happy Hunting*. A Hollywood career failed to soar, though there were flashes of her verve in *There's No Business Like Show Business* (1954), which boasted Donald O'Connor, Dan Dailey, Johnny Ray, Mitzi Gaynor, and Marilyn Monroe in its cast, and Irving Berlin as its composer.

So the opportune moment arrived in 1958, while she was keeping busy with television appearances with Perry Como, Eddie Fisher, and Dinah Shore, and struggling in a bad marriage to Robert Six. Merman remembers that when she received Laurents's draft of *Gypsy*, she knew immediately that Mama Rose was an actress's dream. Ever since Joshua Logan had given her a little trophy inscribed "To Sarah Bernhardt Jr." for her comic hussy in *Stars in Your Eyes*, she had known she could act. Now she'd have a chance to prove it. Merman stated in her autobiography: "In most musicals there is a hairline story, a thin plot and thinner characterizations. *Gypsy* was a full-fledged play. It could have dispensed with the music." She didn't think twice about accepting the opportunity, although she insisted on a personal dresser, hair-stylist, first-class accommodation, the top dressing-room, a salary of $3,000 a week, and additional perquisites for any cast recording. Moreover, she was made production partner who would receive "5 percent until initial costs were recouped and 7 percent of the gross thereafter."

A free adaptation of Gypsy Rose Lee's memoir, Laurents's script still stands on its own — without the magnificent score — as a credible, impressionistic collage of dying vaudeville and small-time burlesque during the twenties and thirties, while at the same time being much more than flashes of these old-style entertainments.

Before actually starting his libretto, Laurents spoke with Gypsy Rose Lee and realized from things she said that she had invented most of her memoir for public consumption. Stephen Sondheim relates that every time Laurents returned to talk to her, "she had a different account of how she got into vaudeville, how she got into burlesque, etc. So he decided he might as well make up his own story." This presented no problem to Gypsy, who insisted on only one thing: the title had to be Gypsy. She didn't care about anything else. "As a matter of fact," Laurents recalls, "when she saw the script and read the part about Herbie, the mother's boy friend, she said, 'God, I wish I had thought of that for my autobiography!' " When Laurents pressed her to explain how she got the name "Gypsy," she exclaimed, "Oh, honey, I've given fourteen or fifteen versions. Yours will be as good as mine."

The only legal complication about the literary property was in obtaining the release-form of June Havoc, Gypsy's younger sister. Leland Hayward invited Laurents to Stratford, Connecticut, where Havoc was playing Titania in A Midsummer Night's Dream. They visited her backstage and then in her home, and during all this, she did not remove her stage make-up, sequins, or head-dress. Theodore Taylor relates that they were startled when she scolded them for arriving late at the performance. "You were late, but of course, you didn't come to see my performance, only to get my name on that piece of paper."

She behaved capriciously, acting charming one moment, angry the next. Her sister's memoir, she said, was a wonderful book, but moments later she reversed herself. "It's a vulgar book. You're supposed to be a playwright," she upbraided Laurents. "Why do you want to make a play of this?" "I find it touching," he replied. "I'm touching," she declared. "Not her. She's cheap. She eats out of tin cans."

The former pocket-sized Pavlova had really been terribly hurt by her elder sister's book, for she felt that the memoir exploited their childhood for ill gain and, worse, had often resorted to complete fabrication for the sake of a laugh or good anecdote. She could have sought legal redress, but knowing how hard Gypsy had worked on the book, she had let the matter slide, according to Preminger — "almost as a gift, sister to sister." But the play was a different matter altogether for it involved strangers — not blood relatives — and Havoc saw no reason to allow any further exploitation and blackening of her past. The script, she complained, had made her look like an untalented whiner who simply grabbed her boyfriend and ran. Gypsy had begged her: "It's my monument. . . . It doesn't have to be factual, it only has to be big, exciting, and — and a smash!" "You were never a pathetic Cinderella," Havoc had objected. "They can't make a musical out of that, June."

But Havoc was not willing to be passive about any more falsifications of her childhood and adolescence. Fable time, gossip time, and make-a-buck time were not going to happen any longer without a fight from her.

Hayward and Laurents came away from their visit without her release. But the script and character of Baby June went ahead anyway.

Gypsy was a special challenge to Laurents — not simply because the anecdotes were so rich, so plenteous, and so diverting in a scattered way, but because he resisted the easy temptation to turn his libretto into a variation of the familiar rags-to-riches Cinderella tale. Nor did he want to make his libretto a backstage saga about a domineering mother. "This woman is a classic," he commented. "What we've got here is a mother who has to learn that if you try to live your children's lives, you'll end up by destroying yourself."

There is still a Cinderella quality in the musical, made ever so meretriciously glamorous by the tinselled gaudiness of small-time vaudeville and big-time burlesque. Moreover, Louise begins as the ungainly "Plug" or untalented sister of Baby June, but she fulfills her mother's dream of big-time success. But the musical undercuts the whimsy and fairy-tale wish-fulfillment by taut, lean, pungent reality that becomes apparent to the audience, if not quite to Mama Rose, the formidable dreamer who suddenly discovers that she cannot dream her children into a false paradise. More than this, she also learns that they have finally outgrown her.

The play opens in a tacky vaudeville theatre in Seattle, where "Uncle Jocko's Kiddie Show" is in rehearsal and packed with children in horrible, homemade costumes. Mama Rose barges in, calling out instructions and encouragement to her two darlings, and delicately shoving aside Jocko while dispensing platitudes and bromides that enshrine her own erect will and drive: "God helps him who helps himself." She comes across like a demoniacally possessed stage-mother, but her gaiety and confidence are disarming. Charging Jocko with playing favourites, she advances, *"hatpin extended like Joan of Arc's sword,"* upon a Balloon Girl who monopolizes the stage. And as her own daughters watch in amusement, the music blares and there is a blackout.

The blackout — which is a technique used throughout the play — freezes the image of a militant, charging mother, prepared to undertake any gambit in the interests of her own children. And in Scene 2, this mama is busy dreaming up "a whole new act" called "Baby June and Her Newsboys." Assured that "God's like me" — for He and Mama Rose both need "outside assistance" — she brushes off a second intimation (her father's) that she's crazy. Though she cannot squeeze any more money out of him, she will not agree to his urging to stay in Seattle, abandon her delusive dream, and marry yet again. After three husbands, she's "through with marriage." Her dreams, she insists, are "real dreams" and she's going to make them "come real" for her girls. Unlike other women who would be content to settle down, she cannot abide sitting still. She will fight to get out of any place that requires her to sit away her life or her daughters' futures. And it is now that the gypsy motif establishes itself. Rose spins a virtually mythic genesis-story about and for Louise: "You were born with a caul. That means you got powers to read palms and tell fortunes and wonderful things are going to happen to you!" Who knows if the caul is fabrication, for Mama Rose has already put a special mark on the elder girl and announced the advent of wonderful things. Her own father brands her a gypsy for "running around the country," but she rehearses her catechism of deliverance through dreams.

The next scene shows us Rose's spontaneous recruitment of

youngsters while she is in transit to Los Angeles. It is pure vaudeville and emblematically semaphored by revue-sketch cutout props, placards, and banner. Nothing is allowed to get in the way of Rose's story or goal.

Herbie, her foil, appears in the next scene. A version of the memoir's Sam Gordon, the mysterious stranger who just walks into the lives of the Hovicks and becomes their business manager, Herbie does not have the faintest tinge of strangeness about him. Described in the stage directions as being *"nice-looking"* and as having *"a sweetly sad, tired quality,"* he is nothing more than a good-natured candy salesman and the exact antithesis of Rose, who appears to him to be *"a pioneer woman without a frontier."* The two are opposites that are attracted to each other, and Rose is perceptive and articulate enough to express this paradoxical affinity: "I like you — but I don't want marriage. You like me — but you don't want show business." Their fundamental outlooks on life are also quite different, for as Rose says: "You look at what we don't have, I look at what we do have."

Scene 5 is concerned with the new act in Los Angeles: Baby June and her Newsboys, with a cornily patriotic finish as June, dressed like a red, white, and blue Statue of Liberty, twirls batons *"for all she is worth,"* while behind her, the American Eagle pops up over the newspaper kiosk and the band plays "The Stars and Stripes." But the value of this florid scene is in the sense of transition it provides: *"As the music builds and gets faster, the name of the city on the illuminated placard changes. It goes from one town to another, finally winding up with* AKRON.*"* During this, however, there is a dramatic change in the characters: Louise and June and her Boys seem to grow larger in the flickering dissolve and are replaced on stage by older actors, all in the same costumes as the originals, but now representations of the characters at an older age.

The dream-like dissolve connects the plot to the dream motif as well, and this is especially relevant for the very next scene is about Rose's comic dream about a performing cow. This dream supplies her with the idea for her next vaudeville act. But Scene 6 is wildly farcical as Rose, fearful of being evicted by the pompous hotel manager who charges her with harbouring pets and other unregistered persons, feigns being a victim of sexual assault by him. The ensuing commotion is interrupted by Herbie's arrival with Mr. Goldstone, the Orpheum agent, who has booked the act on his circuit. All at once, Mama Rose's crazy dream has found its opportune moment of realization — though we must wait for Scene 8 to see this barnyard vaudeville in its absurd hayseed glory.

Scene 7 is set in a gaudy Chinese restaurant, where Rose and her girls arrive in coats made from their hotel blankets. This scene makes it quite clear that Rose will not marry Herbie, although her excuse has nothing to do with a question of his suitability. Rose's dream for June — "Just let me get June's name up in lights so big, they'll last my whole life" — is the reason why other personal issues must be postponed or dropped altogether. So totally committed to this dream is she that she fails to take her suitor at his word: "If I ever let loose, it'll end with me picking up and walking." Rose shrugs this off with a joke but she misses the man's sincerity. She is still more afraid of sitting still and dying than of losing a man who stands up for her. The psychological undertone here is dark and there is irony in Rose's fierce confidence that neither the dream nor Herbie will get away from her.

The dark undertone deepens in the next scene where June, no longer the baby her mother determinedly tries to keep as such, releases her cold anger at the act. In essence, of course, it is an anger whose real target is her mother. While she and her sister both acknowledge their mother's indomitable drive, they also hint at the invidious aspect of her singlemindedness. As June puts it: "Momma can do one thing: she can make herself believe anything she makes up." In the instant, however, the girls transfer their anger to Herbie, while wishing that their mother would simply marry "a plain man" so that they could all enjoy the closeness and unity of a normal family. But Louise, who voices these sentiments, makes up her own dreams, and although she does not have her mother's invincible belief in herself and her own power of self-fulfillment, she does have an intense yearning — as is shown by the end of the next scene when she visualizes herself as Tulsa's partner and gets him to dance with her.

Act I ends with a scene that could potentially lead to Rose's devastation. On an Omaha railroad platform, she learns through a letter from June that her daughter has secretly married Tulsa (Laurents's substitute for the real-life Bobby) and taken off with him. For a moment she is stunned enough to become a zombie, but then she emerges from her trance, and shows that she is the strongest character in the story. She merely brushes aside June's disappearance and shifts her focus to Louise, vowing to make her a star. The death of one dream simply begets a new dream. Mama Rose becomes a superwoman at this moment — one who refuses to be violated by any sense of desolation or defeatism. What could have been a moment of utter loss and emptiness is turned, by her superhuman determination and bravado, into a supreme apocalypse of her violent, transcendental optimism. It is a stunning climax, and she translates the moment into a sheer performance of vital joyousness. While Herbie and Louise stand silent and benumbed, she merely plows onward. But there is a special twist here, for the sheer force of her declaration runs counter to common sense and reality, and the silent witness of Herbie and Louise is in counterpoint to her roaring gallantry. Is she a sane dreamer or a sadly mistaken one? The question can only be posed, not answered, at this point. Suffice it to say that she staves off self-pity as well as our pathos for her, though there is a poignancy in the fact that nobody else on stage with her shares her vision or regenerated strength.

The opening of Act II almost mocks this vision and strength by presenting a ghastly new act in Texas, "Madam Rose's Toreadorables," in which the only Spanish accents are in the music and the bad senorita costumes, especially Louise's gaudy toreador outfit. Otherwise the lyrics are identical with those for the earlier vaudeville acts.

The burlesque portion of the musical begins backstage in a large Wichita theatre dressing-room, crowded with photos and junk, and where bawdy strippers rehearse their gimmicks. The air could turn blue with some of their double-entendres, and Rose quickly loses her excitement over being "back in a real theatre." For a brief while she becomes a female Micawber, expecting "Something'll turn up," but she knows that this likelihood is slim. It is a vulnerable time for her and just once does she admit to pessimism. In a moment of weakness she asks Herbie to marry her, reversing the pattern that has so far dominated their relationship. Ironically, it is he, this time, who procrastinates: "The day we close." All through this scene we sense the death of a dream — and the word "dream" is re-introduced as a leitmotif, although in a somewhat sad mode. The strategic importance of this scene is to prompt Rose into reactivating her dream, force her into contradicting herself eventually, and cueing her with words that will vibrate in her fanciful imagination. First prompt is the happy accidental birth of the nickname "Gypsy" for Rose Louise. But a bigger prompt is in the common theme of the three lead strippers — gimmickry. Mazeppa bumps and grinds to the accompaniment of her trumpet. Electra performs with electric lights illuminating her body's strategic points. And Tessie does a broken-down ballet leading into unrefined burlesque. All her life, Mama Rose has dreamed up gimmicks for her performing daughters, and she can certainly be counted upon to learn a lesson from the strippers.

Scene 3, the briefest in the show, is a scene on the run: in a backstage corridor, stagehands are busy with lighting adjustments, and Amanda (Agnes) is about to bid farewell to her stage career while being caught in some of the bustling preparation for Herbie's marriage to Rose. Amanda is to serve as bridesmaid before returning to her hometown, and this fragment of a scene underscores a twinge of regret on her part, as well as the small theme of a return to normalcy. The scene flashes past and provides comic relief before a heavily dramatic moment.

Scene 4 is pivotal to the second-half of *Gypsy*. It begins in an empty dressing-room which looks even emptier now that most of Rose's belongings have been packed. While a production number is heard continuously under the scene, the action unfolds in stirring mixtures of comedy, heartache, and exaltation. Herbie is excited by the fact that Rose is finally about to marry him, but she is very subdued. Nervously, Louise never takes her eyes off her mother, just in case she might miss the slightest sign of vacillation or a surprising change of mind. The comedy of Herbie's garrulous excitement accordingly acquires a nervous edge. He knows that he ought to stop babbling or burbling but he's so happy that he cannot. "I'm finally getting everything I wanted!" he exclaims joyously. But this assurance is undercut by the uncharacteristically subdued demeanour of Rose and by Louise's silent watchfulness. Then the first concrete lead-in to the anticipated *volte-face* in Rose occurs: the star stripper has been arrested for soliciting, and as she is the novelty, the main attraction can't be provided to the clientele. At this point, Rose is standing dead still, but with her ears and mind hypersensitive to the vibrating possibilities inherent in this unexpected circumstance. "My daughter can do it," she offers boldly, but steps back *"as though afraid of herself."* This stage-direction is crucial to understanding her complex psychology. She is not a mere grotesque — not the clichéd heartless stage-mother. This Rose is hard-boiled, to be sure, but subject to fear of her own powers. We feel that in the long speech that soon follows she needs a justification more for herself than for Louise or Herbie. "I knew something would turn up! . . . Oh, silly, you're not really gonna strip! All you'll do is walk around the stage in time to the music and drop a shoulder strap at the end. . . . I promised my daughter we'd be a star!"

The speech is rampant with apologies in the classical sense of self-justifying arguments. The pronoun shifts ("I," "you," "we") trace the peculiar dynamic by which Rose functions. As Herbie and Louise *"stand dead still, watching,"* she exercises her entire repertoire of excuses and triumphant vindications in passionately charged rhetoric. Now that stardom — even though contaminated and diminished by a burlesque environment — is so close at hand, she can conveniently put aside her moral scruples (hard to think she has any which are deep-rooted!) and seize the opportunity. *Carpe diem* is her implicit attitude, but is she really doing all this for Louise? The question is probably a rhetorical one, given the organic and seamless manner in which she unites herself with her daughter as if both were to share one and the same success. Her dream may truly be for her daughter's welfare, but Rose is attached herself to the dream and is one with it.

So driven is she that all other matters are swept aside. The marriage can wait, she feels, as she pushes Tessie the Twirler's gift of long white gloves into Louise's service. June's "Let Me Entertain You" number is pressed into service as well, and Rose supplies snippets of the burlesque technique her daughter should use to make her new act grand and elegant. She does not believe Herbie when he tells her that there will be no marriage for them — not in the morning or ever! Herbie now refuses to crawl after her. He still loves her but knows that his love is doomed by her commitment to an unreal dream. She apologizes, she angrily accuses him of "killing" her out of jealousy because the girls come first. But Herbie, for the first time in their unsteady and uneven relationship, answers back and scores the most telling points. He indicates that Rose has deluded herself into believing that everything she does is for her daughters' unequivocal good. "Then why did June leave? . . . She didn't want the act any more than Louise wants this! . . . She'll leave like June did!" His words reverberate with possible dramatic ironies which Rose refuses to acknowledge. In fact, she never has a satisfactory retort for any of Herbie's more probing questions. Where is Rose going to be when Louise is a star? Where is Rose going to be when Louise is married? Rose can offer only a wish-fulfillment fantasy: "She won't be getting married for years — she's a baby!" But this defiance flies in the face of reasonableness. It also betrays her inability to know herself or her daughters whom she has perpetually circumscribed by a myth of childlike purity and innocence.

There is a poignant moment when she asks "Herbie . . . why does everybody walk out?" as he picks up his suitcase to leave. Herbie permits himself only one gesture of sympathy: he pats her shoulder. *"Without looking up, she reaches for his hand and holds it there."* Then she pleads with him not to leave because she needs him. "What for?" he counters, and their next exchange puts the capper on their relationship:

ROSE: A million things.
HERBIE: Just one would be better. Good-bye, honey.
  (*Silence. He kisses the top of her head*) Be a good girl.
  (*Quietly, he goes out the door. Music starts*)
ROSE: You go to hell!

47

This dialogue is fraught with psychological ramifications. Rose is vague about the reasons for her need because she does not really have a need beyond ego-stroking or comfort when she is low-spirited. It is clear that she does not need Herbie as a man to look up to, because she is unable to look up to anyone. Her major focus is on her dream of success. Not attuned to the vibrations of a deep, committed relationship with the only man who apparently cares for her, she lacks emotional maturity. She is a perverse woman-child in her own way, and Herbie signals this by his kiss to the top of her head and by his admonition: "Be a good girl." His wording is best suited to a parent addressing a child. Feeling somewhat patronized, Rose explodes in a curse, and this, too, is symptomatic of childish immaturity. Unable to get her way with this man, she can resort only to an execration. And then, true to her singleminded purpose, she prepares for Louise's launching as a new burlesque star. There is, however, one new note in her chord of defiance — an anguish at having driven Herbie to do the one thing she had always assumed to have been beyond his willpower. She is alone again — left to her own resources.

The rest of this scene is also pivotal — but now for Louise. The once ungainly "Plug," who had always been the untalented half of the Hovick duo, she is left alone before a long mirror in the dressing-room. As dark figures scurry through the corridor outside and make diverse comments, chiefly negative, about her chances of success, she examines herself closely in the mirror before very gently, almost tentatively, awakening to the possibilities for herself. She discovers a latent beauty and grand pride, and this moment of self-discovery is achieved solely through mime and just prior to her first striptease performance. She becomes, in effect, the Cinderella in Rose's dream. The rest of the scene builds upon her novelty as a stripper who teases more than strips in a series of vignettes that move from Detroit to Philadelphia to New York. The visual climax is at Minsky's, where in *"a garish, loud, corny production number with nudes on a Christmas tree and slithering show girls,"* she emerges from a wrapped Christmas present, brought on by clowns dressed as Santa Claus. Her diamond-pure elegance glitters tantalizingly as she pulls the curtain across the stage with her, shutting out everything but the memory of herself.

The placard for the penultimate scene is entitled "Mother's Day." The disarray and vulgarity of the dressing-room immediately radiates a negative feeling, and the unfolding action confirms the irony in the title placard. Meddlesome Rose is prohibited from going backstage at this theatre — a prohibition of Louise's making — but this does not stop her from trying to dress up the wall of the room with the prop Cow's head or to continue her nagging. She expects vaudeville to revive and warns Gypsy that she won't be ready when this revival occurs. The nub of this scene, however, isn't in the mother's nagging or complaints, or even simply in Gypsy's celebrity. The real crux is in the schism between mother and daughter. It becomes plain from Gypsy's French lessons, maids, press agents, photograph session in the bathtub for *Vogue*, and her "fancy friends with their fancy parties" that she has been transformed into a woman who makes her own decisions and who finally can live her own life without outside interference. Such a transformation has evidently created a distance between her and Rose — which is something Rose shows first with bitterness and then with a wry attempt to shame her daughter. Carried away by bitterness, she denigrates Gypsy's "lousy French" and pretensions at literacy. Hurt at being kept away from her daughter's friends and their parties, she cries: "You know what you are to them? A circus freak! This year's novelty act!"

Rose, however, does not get away with her attack this time, for Gypsy summons up all her own fiery anger in response. Nobody laughs at her, because she laughs first. And she exults in the fact that she, a girl from Seattle, with no formal education and no obvious talent, has become a star. And she enjoys this life she now has because whatever it is, it is her own and nobody is going to take it away from her. This speech is delivered with such blazing vehemence that Rose is clearly stunned. Mama would prefer to drop the subject, but Gypsy insists on finishing the issue. Rose still wants to believe that Gypsy needs her, that Gypsy is still somehow a child bound to her mother. When Gypsy cries out: *"Momma, you have to let go of me!"* Rose finds it hard to take in the full implications of her words. It is a devastating moment for the proud "jungle" mother and it forces her to wonder aloud for the first time in her rough-and-tumble life what she has lived her life for. The self-questioning is not done to milk emotion but to declare her aching devastation:

All the working and pushing and fenagling. . . . All the scheming and scrimping and lying awake nights figuring: how do we get from one town to the next? How do we all eat on a buck? How do I make an act out of nothing? What'd I do it for? You say I fought my whole life. I fought *your* whole life. So now tell me: *what'd I do it for?*

It is just possible that she is aching to be told that she has struggled, schemed, and fought for her daughter. This, in any case, is how Gypsy reads the question, for she responds quietly after a long pause: "I thought you did it for me, Momma." Is this an honest response or a half-truth? Has Rose been guilty of appropriating her daughters' lives as her own property? Or has she craftily deceived everybody into thinking that she has sacrificed her own independence all for selfless love of her children? In other words, the key question of the play is whether Rose is martyr or monster.

The answer is that she has been part martyr, part monster, but always a child who grows up wise only after her own children have earned their respective wisdoms. This, at least, is the sense that emerges from the final scene in which Rose delivers her climactic monologue — her single most glorious aria. As a lone spotlight picks up her form as she moves downstage, and she has the entire bare stage to herself, except for a few stacked flats of scenery used earlier in a big production number, her mind races through her life story and her soul pours out her most heartfelt anger, defiance, and exaltation. This is her biggest private moment, her cry from the heart, and, ultimately, her turn to get a dream all for herself. But after the noisy bravado and sheer defiance, she acknowledges: "I guess I did do it for me." Now she is an abashed child, and Gypsy, who enters quietly, recognizes this and holds out her arms to Rose like a mother offering consolation and refuge to a child. Then it is the daughter who makes it up to the mother, inviting her to a friend's party and offering Rose her own mink. The sentimentality of the ending is quickly blocked and diverted by Rose's final action. She has had another dream, she says, about an advertisement for Minsky's, and tracing her own name first in the air, she notices Gypsy's look, catches herself in her old egomania, and yields top billing in her own fantasy to her daughter. At the curtain, it is the mother who is subordinated at last and subject to reality.

This descriptive analysis of the script, quite independent of the songs and music, should provide some sense of the acute psychological characterization at work — at least in the case of Rose who, to all intents and purposes, is the most vividly drawn, rounded person in the play. It is really because of her personality that the play remains coherent, for her outrageousness is the only consistent tone in the script. Each scene appears to have a different key or colour: the first one is vaudevillian; the second musical comedy; the third farce; and so on. There is plenty of tough drama, some romance. So the play shifts in style and tone, but this inconsistency never has a negative effect on the shape of the story, and the strongest reason is Rose, whose attitude dominates the entire play and carries her audience along on her remarkable journey.

Laurents's script stands solidly on its own merits, even without the magnificent support of Jule Styne's music or Stephen Sondheim's lyrics. It shows clearly that the playwright is not condescending about musicals. It does not try to get away with trite characterizations or situations (though there are some), and it does not strive after an imperial autonomy as a piece of writing. Laurents himself once remarked that a writer has to be prepared to sacrifice ego when composing a libretto: "You have to know that the music is the most important thing and everything has to be built toward it." Laurents did not agree when Sondheim told him that the script could be a play on its own. "Never. Not the way I wrote it. It's too big. The characters are overblown, the strokes are too bold and too broad. It's the presence of music that supports it." Laurents was not being unduly modest: everything in *Gypsy* was made to lead to a strong song. The dialogue is thin by standards of a straight play, but this is a deliberate economy, for in a musical situation and character are filled out by song. All the same, the level of *Gypsy* is much higher than that of the usual Broadway musical of its day. The emotions are big, and the writing never loses contact with reality or human truth. Without Laurents's book, Sondheim would not have had the solid underpinning for his songs, which are extensions of the characters' emotions. Where in *West Side Story*, Laurents had invented a powerful street language that was used dramatically in order to convey a sense of rough gang life, his language in *Gypsy* is colloquial and not at all stylized. None of it can be sacrificed without damaging in some way the pungent drive of the story or the musical comedy world that feeds it and is satirized in the bargain. Indeed, there are trite gags, corny vaudeville moments, and stock characters, but *Gypsy* is rooted in an old-style world, and its characters reflect the tastes and attitudes of their own times. Fading vaudeville and sleazy burlesque give Laurents an opportunity to feed into a tragicomic story of misguided, misjudged mother love. The final three scenes reveal a delicate balance, for with just the slightest tilt, the merest shift in pace or focus, *Gypsy* could easily become musical tragedy. That it is able to entertain while still casting shadows across its central characters' souls is a testament to Arthur Laurents's skill.

Left to right: Sandra Church, Ethel Merman, Jacqueline Mayro.

PHOTO BY FRED FEHL, COURTESY OF THE NEW YORK PUBLIC LIBRARY FOR THE PERFORMING ARTS

PHOTO BY FRED FEHL, COURTESY OF THE NEW YORK PUBLIC LIBRARY FOR THE PERFORMING ARTS

Left to right: Sandra Church, Ethel Merman, Jack Klugman.

Left to right: Chotzi Foley, Maria Karnilova, Faith Dane.

Left to right: Jack Klugman and Ethel Merman.

Ethel Merman.

Back, left to right: Gene Castle, Steve Curry,
Billy Harris, Karen Moore.   Front: Jacqueline Mayro

Sandra Church.

Sandra Church and Ethel Merman.

PHOTO BY FRED FEHL, COURTESY OF THE NEW YORK
PUBLIC LIBRARY FOR THE PERFORMING ARTS

Styne and Sondheim

IRVING BERLIN read Gypsy Rose Lee's book and then declined Merrick and Hayward's offer to do the score for the musical. The producers next approached Cole Porter, who was seriously ill at the time. According to Otis L. Guernsey, they believed that this project might revive him, but he also declined. Soon there was a growing list of auditioning or petitioning songwriters such as Cy Coleman and Carolyn Leigh, Marshall Barer and Dean Fuller, but without concrete results. Part of the difficulty was that nobody — not even the producers or librettist — knew just what sort of music was required for the book. Then, just before Jerome Robbins departed for Europe for a summer holiday, Stephen Sondheim handed him the first three songs he had written for *A Funny Thing Happened on the Way to the Forum*. Robbins was so thrilled by their quality that he contacted Leland Hayward and asked that Sondheim do the score for *Gypsy*. "Of course I was thrilled," comments Sondheim," — until Ethel Merman announced that she would not take a chance on an unknown composer . . . that she'd be perfectly happy to have me do the lyrics, but she wanted Jule Styne to do the music." Merman's lack of confidence was partly motivated by an unhappy earlier experience with a neophyte lyricist on *Happy Hunting* (1956), but partly because she instinctively knew that her large extrovertive voice and style required a special sort of composition and orchestration that were not yet within Sondheim's experience. "This is not denying Steve's musical talent," adds Jule Styne, "but to write for Ethel Merman was a kind of bag he didn't know much about." Besides, Merman was eager to work with Styne who had been her coach at 20th Century-Fox in the late thirties, and who had been one of her producers in *Anything Goes* and *Panama Hattie*. Merman had always enjoyed their association and said: "The thing I knew about Jule was that his music was singable and commercial. Up to *Gypsy*, I'd only worked with George Gershwin, Cole Porter, and Irving Berlin. And I felt that Jule was perfect for this show. So I insisted on him."

Laurents asked Sondheim if he would be willing to write just the lyrics, but Sondheim, who was trained as a musician and wanted to be a composer, thought of lyric writing as a sideline he had slipped into, partly because of the influence of Oscar Hammerstein, and partly because he had to earn a living. As Guernsey points out, Sondheim really didn't want to wait another couple of years to write a score himself. So he went to his artistic mentor, Hammerstein, who persuaded him to accept the assignment because of the opportunity it provided to work with extraordinarily talented people and particularly because it offered a chance to write a show for a star (which Sondheim had never done before):

We were then in the summer, and the show was set to go into rehearsal in February. Oscar persuaded me that, at the worst, it would be six months out of my life. It would involve some frustration, but it was a chance to write in a whole different vein and for a star. Because I liked the piece enough and because I knew and liked Jule's stuff a lot, I said o.k.

Nevertheless, he was heartsick.

Another heartsick person was Styne. "I was tempted to pick up the phone and call Merrick to say, 'Hey, what about me? Remember, you offered me the job first.' No one can write better for Ethel Merman than I can." As it was, Merrick did call to talk about the problem of trying to please everybody — Merman, Sondheim, Hayward, and Laurents — and urged Styne to be patient.

When Jerome Robbins brought up Styne's name as composer, Arthur Laurents was unenthusiastic: "Jule is a great pop song writer, and he's done some shows, but this is a dramatic entity." This enraged Styne when he heard of it, but Laurents later explained: "I'd never met him. But to my mind, musicals were beginning to take a different turn in the fifties. I knew Jule wrote great 'tunes' but this was a dramatic piece and I didn't know that he was capable of turning out a dramatic score."

Sondheim himself had similar reservations about Styne's appropriateness:

Jule's shows had been in a rather traditional mold — what used to be called "musical comedy," songs and block comedy scenes. I didn't know how he'd adapt to another way of thinking, whether he'd be willing to keep his eyes and ears on character and story rather than hit songs.

Sondheim knew that Laurents wanted a score that would enable him to enlarge the characters and develop them quickly and broadly.

Jerome Robbins was a great booster of Styne, and assured Laurents that he would get the composer to audition. Laurents was aghast: "Oh, it's Jule Styne. You can't ask him to audition for me." But Robbins stated that Styne would willingly do so.

Styne did not show any resentment for having to audition. There was not a question of humility or wounded pride on his part when he and Laurents went to Robbins's apartment on Seventy-fourth Street. Styne played some of his hits. He also played some things that had been cut from *Bells Are Ringing*. Laurents:

"The music had more guts than I thought possible. Listening to it, I realized that this man had a far greater range than I had thought. I also believe that when you work with better people, you become better. So I then readily accepted Jule as the composer."

The perfect collaboration between Styne and Sondheim could not have been predicted on the basis of their respective backgrounds. Born in the Jewish ghetto of Bethnal Green in London's East End on December 31, 1905, Julius Styne (né Stein) learned five or six of Harry Lauder's songs at four and, according to Theodore Taylor, jumped up onto the Hippodrome stage to do an impromptu vocal accompaniment. On the Cunard liner that brought him and his family to the U.S., young Julius discovered that "by singing and jigging for the stewards he could buy his way into first class, a lesson to eventually bear melodic fruit in *Gypsy*'s 'Let Me Entertain You.'" A child prodigy, he played solo piano with the Chicago Symphony at the age of nine, while dressed in a black silk Lord Fauntleroy suit, with lace collar and cuffs, and with his feet barely able to reach the extension pedal of the grand piano. The occasion was actually a competition in which he won a silver medal for a rendition of Haydn's D Major Piano Concerto. A little later, as a soprano in a Jewish choir, he amazed the cantor by being able to distinguish between a F sharp and a F natural. A few days after joining the musician's union — he declared he was sixteen though he looked barely into his teens — he was booked as relief pianist at the Haymarket burlesque house. There he learned how to play grind music for strippers, watched the drummer time the bumps, and absorbed lessons in a form that he would exploit many years later for *High Button Shoes* and *Do Re Mi* (1960). The strippers smothered the baby-faced teenager in their special way by getting up over the lights and bumping straight at his nose. Then backstage, they teased him further by throwing G-strings at him and flicking at his fly.

His teenage years exposed him to ragtime and blues, for the Chicago of his adolescence teemed with contemporary jazzmen. Styne quickly proved his mettle as a jazz pianist, playing in bands with the like of Benny Goodman, Glenn Miller, and Jack Teagarden. By 1923, Chicago was hot with virtuosos who carried jazz to a pinnacle. Louis "Satchmo" Armstrong, King Oliver, "Fats" Waller, Earl "Fatha" Hines, Jimmy Yancey, Bessie Smith, and Ma Rainey were part of Styne's lucky experience, and it is very probable, as Theodore Taylor observes, that "The earthiness of some of Jule Styne's Broadway music . . . dates back to 1923."

The next year, Styne played pit piano for stage shows at the Balaban & Katz theatre chain, and at the age of twenty he became a bandleader, with the dubious distinction of having Al Capone's participation as a "guest" conductor for an evening of George Gershwin. As was the custom of the day, musicians fed off the mob because every club and restaurant was controlled by gangsters. Capone offered to lead the band, and it was an offer, of course, that Styne could not afford to refuse.

When the gang wars became too wild and hot, Styne moved to New York and became a voice coach for girlfriends of the underworld. From the start, he looked upon the coaching as a way to make a living and gain important contacts. By now New York was the home of jazz and big bands. Benny Goodman, the Dorsey brothers, Duke Elllington, Guy Lombardo, Eddy Duchin, and Paul Whiteman were the headliners at hotels, and as Styne continued coaching girls with no evident talent, he could only watch forlornly as other musicians waxed with opportunity. But there were occasional assignments that were diverting — a comic operatic oratorio for the Ritz Brothers at Billy Rose's Casino de Paree, and a taste of the musical stage at Miami Beach. Ironically, his job as vocal coach secured an unexpected reward: he actually improved the hoodlums' girlfriends so much that Hollywood beckoned him out west, where he coached stars at 20th Century-Fox, including Shirley Temple and Alice Faye. The child star intimidated him. She was already at peak glory in 1937, when he took on the unenviable task of polishing her voice and musical arrangements. On the screen, she stole scenes from everybody — whether it was Bill "Bojangles" Robinson or Lionel Barrymore. Off screen, she stole attention and authority from her parents. "Look, I earn all the money in this family," she would scream at her father. "Don't tell me what to do." Almost needless to say, Alice Faye was a marshmallow by comparison.

Styne's ability to knock off easy melodies was discovered in due course. Darryl F. Zanuck, who was head at Fox, said to him after a year: "Jule, you're in a luxury business. You ought to write songs. Have you written a song?" Styne replied that he had written two, but that he thought it was square to write songs. Zanuck disagreed: "No, that is a commodity out here. Coaching people they will eventually do away with, but songs they have to have out here — it's your secondary asset." But Zanuck could not give him the $2,500 a week salary for a songwriter because Styne wasn't one yet, so the producer told him to work at Republic Studios which made cheap musicals and where Zanuck had an important contact. In *They're Playing Our Song*, Max Wilk relates how Zanuck told Styne, "you get $900 a week coaching people, you're going to get $165 a week over there at Republic, but you're going to write songs. You'll be the only one there to write. So just pretend that you're investing, betting on yourself. You're a gambling guy, *bet*."

So Styne duly worked at Republic, where he composed for cowboy royalty, Gene Autry and Roy Rogers. Not that his contribution was artistic or regal: he would write five or six songs for each picture — mainly country-and-western music for cattle, mules, pigs, and dogs. But this ability to handle every assignment showed his flexibility and resourcefulness, and led eventually to his experience with pocket musicals, for in addition to churning out horse operas and action "flicks," Republic copied other studios in doing a share of small-budget musicals. Theodore Taylor relates that when Styne and Frank Loesser drew the assignment for *Sis Hopkins* in 1941, starring Bing Crosby, Judy Canova, and Jerry Colonna, they tacked up huge signs on their door: No Cowboys Allowed. No Horses Allowed. No Gunshots.

Loesser and Styne scored a hit with "Since You" in *Sailors on Leave* (1941), starring Dorothy Lamour, and the next year they enjoyed further success with "I Don't Want to Walk without You" from *Sweater Girl*, a story about a group of college students preparing a musical revue, but with a spot of murder thrown in for measure. According to Styne, it was this song and the slightly risqué "I Said No" that made him and Loesser "hot properties" among Hollywood composers. Loesser was so thrilled by their collaboration that he lured Styne away from Republic to Paramount, where they had some more films together until Loesser joined the army. Styne asked Loesser whom he should team up with next, and was told directly: "You've been spoiled, there's no one like me. If you want someone like me, don't get a clever rhymer, because there is a thing called a rhyming dictionary." Anybody can rhyme, Styne was told, and Wilk relates that Loesser urged him to find a partner who could say "something clever and warm, because you need warm lyrics for your music."

Al Cohen, producer of Sis Hopkins, told Styne about Sammy Cahn who had just broken up from Saul Chaplin. Cahn, who had done the lyrics for several popular hits, including "Bei Mir Bist Du Schoen" for the Andrew Sisters, was looking for a new melodist. At first, Styne did not want to write with him because he felt that Cahn was then merely a rhymer who, instead of going back to his Jewish ethnic simplicity, was trying to become another Johnny Mercer. Cohen said: "You know, Cahn is a talented guy." "Sure, he's talented," Styne replied, "but I just came off Frank Loesser and I want to go further." He kept thinking of Loesser's advice: "Write only with the big ones," and Cahn didn't seem big enough. Cohen informed him that Cahn had more experience than Styne and needed a job. Styne then agreed to team up with the kind, energetic Cahn.

The new pair's first hit was "I've Heard That Song Before" from Carolina Blues (1944), an otherwise silly movie with Kay Kyser as a bandleader trying to raise money for a cruiser through a series of war bond rallies. By then Styne was back with Republic who had offered him a greatly increased fee from what Paramount was paying. Cahn and Styne had great success in the forties: at one point, their songs held the first three places in the Hit Parade. Among the successful titles were "I'll Walk Alone," "It's Magic," "Five Minutes More," and "Time After Time," all written between 1944 and 1948. "At one point, in the mid-forties, we were writing so many hits that it became embarrassing," Styne reminisced. (Styne's solo efforts produced "I Fall in Love Too Easily," "Saturday Night Is the Loneliest Night of the Week," "It's Been a Long Long Time," and "Let It Snow! Let It Snow! Let It Snow!") The pair signed with Columbia Pictures in mid-1943 for a seven-picture deal, giving Columbia its first big movie song hits but completing only three films. Frank Sinatra and Doris Day recorded several of the Cahn-Styne hits, and then Broadway beckoned.

Although their first Broadway experience was an unhappy one, the pair happened upon a funny period piece of a story about a couple of swindlers who arrive in New Jersey to sell swampland as real estate and to fix the upcoming Rutgers-Princeton football game. This story became the basis of High Button Shoes, directed by the redoubtable George Abbott. Though the critics were not ecstatic about the libretto, the show was deemed a success, especially for Nanette Fabray's comedy and for Jerome Robbins's memorable Keystone Kops ballet. Styne did win praise for the ballet music, and the experience of working with hard taskmasters such as Abbott and Robbins was something that stimulated his interest in musical theatre. "I learned more from George Abbott and Jerome Robbins on that show than I could have learned on ten shows with lesser talents." Jerome Robbins remarked to a colleague: "Jule's been bitten, God help him."

Gentlemen Prefer Blondes was his next project. A free adaptation of her own novel, Anita Loos's libretto placed flapper Lorelei Lee and her companion, Dorothy, aboard the *Ile de France* bound for Paris. The script indulged in several romantic and comic romps as Lorelei looked for sugar daddies. Produced by Herman Levin and Oliver Smith, directed by John Wilson, and choreographed by Agnes de Mille, the show had lyrics by Leo Robin and music by Styne. Robin provided a fine testimonial to Styne's talent: "He is more than just a song writer or composer. Basically, Jule is a fine showman. He knows the value of certain material at the right points and plays up those points musically." The 740-performance run on Broadway was sensationalized by Carol Channing, whom Styne had drilled patiently in the numbers and who rewarded his faith in her ability by a whacky, show-stopping performance that was a caricature of all blondes.

Styne was able to stay "hot" on Broadway, despite an extremely brief, disastrous run for *Make a Wish* (1951) and a mediocre reception for *Two on the Aisle* (1951). His next venture was as producer of a superb revival of *Pal Joey* (1952), choreographed by Bob Alton and with Harold Lang and Vivienne Segal giving better performances than had Gene Kelly and Segal herself in the original production. The show was chosen Best Musical by the Critic's Circle, and the Columbia Records cast album was a best-seller and nominated by record-producer Goddard Lieberson as one of the ten best musicals ever recorded.

In 1955 Styne, who had once again become essential to Frank

Sinatra's recording career, won an Oscar (along with Sammy Cahn) for "Three Coins in the Fountain" from the movie of the same name. Previously nominated for "I Don't Want to Walk Without You, Baby," "I'll Walk Alone," "It's Magic," and "It Seems to Me I've Heard That Song Before," he was appreciative of the honour, although he believed that the winning song was not as good as his non-winning nominees of previous years.

Styne produced *Mr. Wonderful* (1956), with music and book by Jerry Bock and with Sammy Davis, Jr. starring in his first Broadway role. Davis shot to stardom, and the show ran for 383 performances but finished in the red. However, Styne followed this up with *Bells Are Ringing* (1956), which reunited him with Comden and Green. This musical was conventional but charming simply because it did not pretend to be anything other than a romantic comedy about a pleasant, well-meaning, but inquisitive telephone-operator who eavesdrops on and meddles with the lives of some of her customers, one of whom happens to be an aspiring playwright and her eventual beau. Comden and Green's clever lyrics drew attention, as did Styne's melodies which ranged from ballads to nostalgic rags, but the biggest sensation was Judy Holliday who had critics and audiences applauding her deft zaniness.

Near the end of the year, David Merrick called with the initial offer for Styne to collaborate with Comden and Green on *Gypsy*.

Stephen Sondheim was a different sort of *wunderkind* than was Styne. Born March 22, 1930, to comfortably upper middle-class Jewish parents in New York, he was a precocious child who, according to Zadan, skipped kindergarten and read the *New York Times* in the first grade. After his parents divorced when he was ten, his mother moved with him to Pennsylvania and packed him off to military school, whose regulations and conventions actually provoked his interest. Music took over his life via his mother's acquaintances in Pennsylvania — the Oscar Hammerstein family. At the time, Hammerstein was working on a musical that was to become the legendary *Oklahoma!* and Sondheim's curiosity and interest were sharpened. At fifteen and now in a Quaker-run school, Sondheim and two classmates wrote a musical about campus life called *By*

George, which he thought the world of until Hammerstein gave him a severe but useful critique about its flaws. Although his ego suffered terribly as Hammerstein delivered his comments, Sondheim came to appreciate the value of a true professional insider's way of analyzing the elements of a musical. "At the risk of hyperbole, I'd say that in that afternoon I learned more about songwriting and the musical theater than most people learn in a lifetime." He was getting the distillation of thirty years of experience, and was being treated like a professional.

Wilk notes that the main thing Hammerstein taught Sondheim was that clarity was what counted. "It's *what* you say first, and *how* you say it second. When I started out writing love songs I would write about stars and trees and dreams and moonlight, the usual songwriter's vocabulary. That's fine if you believe it, but I didn't. Oscar said, 'Say what *you* feel, not what other songwriters feel.' "

Hammerstein also stressed the importance of the opening of a show, for as he remarked: "The first lyric the audience hears, the first song, is what really makes or breaks a show. If you start with the right opening, you can ride for forty-five minutes on the telephone book. On the other hand, if you start off with a wrong one, it's an uphill fight all the way."

Hammerstein was an anomaly: an articulate, tough, totally urbane man who, nevertheless, believed in rhyming games and the sentimentality of "Oh, What a Beautiful Morning!" He proved to be the first great influence on Sondheim:

He taught me how to structure a song like a one-act play, how essential simplicity is, how much every word counts and the importance of content, of saying what you, not what other songwriters, feel, how to build songs, how to introduce character, how to make songs relate to character, how to tell a story, how not to tell a story, the interrelationships between lyric and music — all, of course, from his own point of view.

According to Zadan, Hammerstein advised Sondheim to learn by experience and to write four musicals — each in a different way and with a different purpose. The first was to be an adaptation of any play Sondheim admired. The second was to be an adaptation of a bad play. The third was to be an experiment with a non-dramatic genre — say, a novel or short story. And the fourth was to be entirely original.

Sondheim's course of training with Oscar Hammerstein included a lowly but invaluable stint as general office boy and handyman around the Rodgers and Hammerstein production of *Allegro* (1947), what Gerald Bordman calls "a loose, rambling chronicle recounting the life of an ordinary upper-middle-class professional." He was seventeen at the time, and Hammerstein coaxed him by saying that he could now learn what the real theatre was all about in all its highs and lows, triumph and turmoil.

Sondheim was fortunate, too, in his next teacher, for when he was a music major at Williams College, he studied under Robert Barrow. "Before Barrow I waited for all the tunes to come into my head. I was a romantic. He taught me first to learn the technique and then to put the notes down on paper . . . that's what music is." Sondheim duly won the Hutchinson Prize, a two-year fellowship which he used to become a student of avant-garde composer Milton Babbitt in New York. Sondheim revealed a nimble mind and musicality, although he worked slowly, partly out of laziness and partly because of social and frivolous diversions. He loved attending parties and spending vast amounts of time on creating esoteric games and solving intellectual puzzles. At least, his friends were worth knowing: Harold Prince was one, and Burt Shevelove another.

Through Hammerstein's recommendation, he became a writer for *Topper*, a new television series. This proved lucrative enough for Sondheim to be able to rent an apartment in New York. Next came his first professional job in musical theatre: doing the songs for *Saturday Night*, about a group of youths in Flatbush, 1928, all investing in the stock market. Alas, the project ended when the producer suddenly died. At twenty-five, Stephen Sondheim had not yet reached Broadway, but "he did have the best audition portfolio of any unknown songwriter in town."

The producing team of an upcoming musical version of James M. Cain's *Serenade* invited him to play his score for *Saturday Night*. In his small audience was Arthur Laurents who six months later would begin his experimental adaptation of *Romeo and Juliet* to New York street gang life. The Capulets and Montagues were originally to be rival Jews and Gentiles, but the idea got changed once some virulent gang warfare broke out in Los Angeles between Mexicans and so-called Americans. Laurents and Leonard Bernstein, who were in Hollywood because Bernstein was doing the score for *On the Waterfront*, decided that it was a perfect reason to alter their original conception and turn the gangs into young Latins and an amalgam of white American youth. Bernstein was supposed to be doing the score and lyrics for this gang musical, but because of many other pressing commitments, he wanted a collaborator on the lyrics. Zadan relates that Laurents recommended Sondheim to Bernstein who was impressed by the young composer's work on *Saturday Night*: "I went wild, I thought that he was a real, honest-to-God talent. The music wasn't terribly distinguished — it sounded like anybody's music — but the lyrics didn't sound like anybody's lyrics by any means. Sondheim, however, was not thrilled by the offer to write only the lyrics for the show that was to become *West Side Story* (1957). But Oscar Hammerstein persuaded him to accept because it would be a marvellous opportunity to work with first-rate professionals on a project that was decidedly fresh and interesting. So, Sondheim, swallowing his injured pride, agreed to become lyricist — but not without complaint to several friends and acquaintances: "I can't do this show. . . . I've never been that poor and I've never even *known* a Puerto Rican!"

West Side Story was a landmark musical in several ways. Called "a movement musical" by Richard Kislan because all essential communication of plot, characterization, and theme was through "the physical expression of movement and gesture" where language yielded to dance images, it adapted a tragic Shakespearean romance to contemporary language and dance. It had the shortest libretto of any Broadway musical, for playwright Arthur Laurents realized that Jerome Robbins's conception was such an exciting integration of ideas and feelings with movement that no elaboration of text was either necessary or particularly advantageous. Or to put it in Sondheim's acutely critical way, the show was not so much about people as about a mode of telling a story. The colourful theatricality disguised many of the musical's inherent flaws, and the show eventually won its status as an innovative Broadway musical, though it was not unanimously well received by critics. Sondheim thought the book had purple writing in dialogue and songs and that the characters were one-dimensional. He was dissatisfied with some of his own lyrics, feeling that they were either bloodless or incongruously clever. Yet, he was also aware and appreciative of the fact that more happened in this plot than in that of any other Broadway musical he could name. "Arthur didn't want the show to say something about the human heart; he was interested in having some fun inventing forms for the theater — ways that he could make song, dance, and dialogue blend."

Sondheim did not receive significant critical acclaim. Leonard Bernstein and Jerome Robbins shared most of the plaudits, while Sondheim's name was omitted from Brooks Atkinson's generally favourable review and his lyrics were panned by Walter Kerr. Zadan describes how Sondheim did nevertheless win notoriety, for three days after the show's opening, a *New York Times* article by Dr. Howard A. Rusk charged that one of Sondheim's lyrics slandered Puerto Rico. The line in question referred to Puerto Rico as "island of tropical breezes . . . island of tropical diseases." Dr. Rusk reviewed the prevailing tropical diseases in Puerto Rico — cholera, dengue, filariasis, typhus, yellow fever, and leprosy — and concluded that "no significant disease problems related to its tropical climate." He ended his piece with this didactic point:

Mr. Sondheim's lyrics will probably remain unchanged and Puerto Rico's morbidity and mortality rates will continue to decline. In the meantime, *West Side Story* is a dramatic and effective production and Puerto Rico is a healthy island. Would that we in New York City could find as effective measures to control our social blight of juvenile delinquency as Puerto Rico, island of tropical breezes, has found in controlling its "tropical diseases."

As soon as *West Side Story* settled into its initial Broadway run,

Sondheim invited his old pal Burt Shevelove to collaborate on a show for which Sondheim was to write both words and music. This was to become *A Funny Thing Happened on the Way to the Forum*, but early in 1958, while a first draft of the vaudeville Plautus was being completed, Sondheim received the call to help with *Gypsy*.

Sondheim had first met Styne very casually, at a party in Leonard Bernstein's apartment where Styne played mainly his own pieces on a piano. "I was impressed by the enthusiasm with which Jule attacked the keyboard, and by his nervous good humour." Styne had a reputation for being a compulsive worker. A short, excitable man, he never let up once he undertook a project and he spoke, as Lehman Engel describes, "like a machine gun." Usually positive on everything, he rarely listened to others and sometimes overreacted by screaming when frustrated. However, no negative traits showed as yet to Sondheim.

Their first business meeting for *Gypsy* occurred in a garden apartment (owned by Ruth Dubonnet, one of Styne's close companions). Styne was extremely nervous: "I thought he might hit me over the head, knowing that he wanted to do the whole show. He was young, ambitious and a huge talent. But he was also very gentle, and we got along fine." Styne handed Sondheim thirteen "trunk" songs — pieces from unproduced shows or movies, or pieces cut from earlier shows and that were lying in obscurity in the composer's so-called trunk. Sondheim, however, disappointed him by stating that the material should be fresh in order to suit the particular words and situations of *Gypsy*. Moreover, he made it clear that he could not write words to just notes, and so the two would have to wait for an outline from Laurents.

Neither collaborator knew where Arthur Laurents was in his libretto work. Sondheim urged Styne to break with past custom and write in a different way than he was used to. Sondheim promised to stay in continual contact with Laurents in order to learn what the playwright wanted lyrically. "We should let him decide for us. Then when he gives me an idea, I'll know what song is in Scene One. By the time we've written that, he'll catch up with us and we'll go on to Scene Two."

By his own estimate, Sondheim conversed with Laurents at least twice a day for a period of four months. Sometimes the conversation was about trivial matters, and sometimes it was about "trying to form and shape the piece." And these talks, Guernsey says, were quite apart from any of the meetings that Styne was a part of with either Sondheim or Laurents or both.

The trio would toss around ideas to see where and how the songs would work. Then Laurents would write the scenes, and Styne and Sondheim would write into these. Sondheim liked this arrangement of having Laurents get ahead of him in the writing because he could then imitate the playwright's diction and style.

Sondheim learned that Laurents wanted a musicalization of the first two pages of dialogue, so he and Styne composed "Some People," which was Merman's opening song. Styne played a long, slow strain, with percussive accompaniment, and this became the patter for the "Some People" sequence. Theodore Taylor relates that Sondheim "often wrote a simple quatrain after a visit to Laurents, and then Jule set his music." This was a novel way of working for Styne, who felt thrilled by it because he knew that he was creating work that he had never done before. He marvelled at Sondheim's lyrics which fired his own enthusiasm and raised the quality of his own already distinguished work. Sondheim knew just what sort of word would fit each note. When Styne's music soared, Sondheim knew that he needed to say something as important as the notes. He never asked for extra notes, and he did not put full value on the rhyme, like most lyricists. "The thought is the main thing with Steve. In most cases, I wrote the music first, and then he wrote the lyrics. Steve said that the music must set the character as well as the words."

As well as the two artists harmonized together, there were dramatic differences in their working rhythms and temperaments. Sondheim worked slowly and laboriously, and liked to feel discouraged at first — if only to challenge himself to greater lyrical heights. Styne, on the other hand, teemed with ideas which were quickly put to music. He was so fertile that he could whip up a second idea soon after scrapping the first. He preferred to write something brand new rather than revise a song that had good potential. It was not a matter of laziness but of brilliant facility, for Styne appeared to assume that if he wrote enough melodies, one of them was sure to be good. Sondheim was amazed at Styne's incredible creative fertility: "He's profligate. If Lenny [Bernstein] makes the most out of the least, then the opposite is true of Jule. He's the least economical composer I know." But some of his old "trunk" songs did get into the show. One of them was "Little Lamb," sung by Louise in her bedroom in Act I, Scene 6, after the girl has been sadly forgotten on her birthday in all the hullabaloo with Mr. Goldstone. Surrounded by her toy animals, and holding her real pet lamb, she sings regretfully and sensitively of the passage of time and of her own forlorn wish for love. It is a sentimental ballad, but one tinted with her vulnerability. She is older in understanding than is her mother, as the wistfulness of the conclusion makes clear: "I wonder how old I am." Coming as it does after the raucous "Mr. Goldstone, I Love You," in which the mild-mannered Orpheum circuit agent is swamped by Rose's flattering attention, "Little Lamb" is a soft, simple, heart-warming ballad. Jerome Robbins did not like it, but yielded to Styne and Laurents in the matter.

Another rescued "trunk" song was "You'll Never Get Away from Me," sung by Mama Rose and Herbie in Act I. Originally written for Marilyn Monroe in *Pink Tights*, it had languished in Styne's trunk for five years, though it did appear in a different guise, under a different title and with different lyrics in *Ruggles of Red Gap*. Sondheim was shocked and upset to learn of this long after *Gypsy* had opened: "If I'd known it had been used in *Ruggles*, I wouldn't have set the lyrics." But all this was after the fact — and the simple fact was that it did work well in *Gypsy*. Really a dialogue in spoken song, it is a duet for Herbie and Rose, but Rose, of course, dominates.

A third "trunk" song was the melody for "Everything's Coming Up Roses." The original melody (called "In Betwixt and Between") had been created for *High Button Shoes*, with lyrics by Sammy Cahn. Jerome Robbins remembered the tune and suggested its use. In *Gypsy* the music needed "a new and easy release, though, because Merman had to rest on it," which must have made Sondheim realize that Styne was a craftsman who knew the singer's voice and how not to overtax it. Sondheim could have composed the lyrics without any particular singer in mind because he was concentrating on characterization. It was Styne who was catering to Merman's voice.

According to Guernsey, "Everything's Coming Up Roses" did present a problem to Sondheim because he had to find a way of topping Laurents's script. Not in the sense of competing with it, but in the sense of soaring off it. It started with "a verse which has no rhythm in it at all," and it led to the opening notes of the main section. Sondheim thought that "The most wonderful thing about that tune at that spot is that it starts at the top of its register. 'You'll be swell, you'll be great. . . .' " Sondheim decided to use "the front part of the melody" and to find a title that would be "at the end of the quatrain, not the beginning."

It took him a week to find the title, and when he did, it baffled Jerome Robbins. "I don't understand that title," the director complained. Sondheim was startled: after all, he had invented a phrase that meant "things are going to be better than ever" and he had done so in a way that wasn't so poetic as to be anomalous with Rose's street jargon, and in a way that seemed "as if it had been in the language for years but was, in fact, invented for that show." "I just don't understand that title," Robbins said. "Why not, Jerry?" "Everything's coming up Rose's *what?*" "I'll tell you what, Jerry. If anybody else has that confusion — anybody connected with the production, in the audience, any of your relatives — I will change the title."

Nobody else was confused, so the title stayed intact, and Merman wept for joy when she first heard the song. Sondheim made every word count, though he knew that there was very little to say in the lyrics after the title was over. So he decided to convey the song's feeling by restricting himself to images of travelling, children, and show business — especially as "the scene was a railroad station and about a mother pushing her child into show business."

Sondheim did not know Merman's acting ability, so he wrote his lyrics in a manner made to exploit her personality. Arthur Laurents had written a speech that kept building powerfully, so what could top that? Sondheim was unsure whether Merman could handle it, so he decided to compose the type of song that the star had been identified with for twenty-five years. " 'Everything's Coming Up Roses' taken out of context is merely another 'Blow, Gabriel, Blow.' It's a song about nothing except a certain feeling with some images in it. Essentially it's a performer song. Little did we know that she was a *wonderful* actress, which only made the moment richer." But there was luck in all this simply because Sondheim knew just how powerful a belter Merman was. "When you write for a musical comedy star, you write for not just the character but the character played by that personality. This is a lesson that has stood me in very good stead ever since."

But clashes of temperament did break out sometimes. Milton Babbitt recalls that Sondheim would get angry with Styne "every once in a while. . . . After all, Jule does not exactly have Steve's sophisticated ambitions. For example, I remember that Steve was very excited about the triplets in 'Everything's Coming Up Roses,' and Jule didn't even know how to notate them. And, of course, Ethel Merman never sang them correctly." Sondheim's attention to detail was sometimes uncompromising. For "Small World," he had written: "Lucky, I'm a woman with children. . . ." Styne gasped because such a lyric would mean that no male could ever sing or record the song. "So?" responded Sondheim, who refused to change the line.

The cleverness of the composition is shown even in three relatively minor songs in Act I. "Small World" is pretty, funny, touching, and cunning because as Rose sings to Herbie about their similarities despite differences, we note how quickly she moves from A to Z in order to hook him as a life-partner. Another clever touch lies in the way in which Rose expands the idea of a "small world" to encompass Herbie and everything else she likes. It is a small song but the lyrical impulse suggests her power to dominate a situation. An additional brilliance is the shifting pace and rhyme: "We have so much in common, / It's a phenomenon. / We could pool our resources / By joining forces / From now on."

"If Mama Was Married," sung by June and Louise in Scene 9 as a wish-fulfillment fantasy, went through three different kinds of song. One version was too polite; another brassy; only the third was right. The song deftly characterizes the juvenescence of June, the maturation of Louise, and the erratic romantic record of Rose, and it does so with lilting satire. The girls both have fun at their mother's expense, mocking her show biz exhortations and personal foibles. Guernsey observes that there is a musical device that comes out of the release, and consists of two bars that follow one of the biggest laughs in the song.

For elegance — though it is elegance in a virtually lost cause — there is "All I Need Is the Girl," something that Styne called a Fred Astaire song. Sung and danced by Tulsa (June's teen suitor), it is a show-off number by a second-rate or even third-rate hoofer. So the irony is that debonair beauty is bestowed on a callow apprentice. Rhythmically, it moves from gentle, careful tap to quick steps, brassy exhibitionism, followed by romantic largo. Lush strings then give it sweep, and it concludes with a glissando of strings after a full orchestral tone.

Laurents helped Sondheim by his notion of subtext. For example, for "Some People," he gave Sondheim the idea that Rose wanted both a $88 plaque on her father's wall as well as a solid means of escape out of the constricting world she came from. The song, therefore, did not become a mere "list song about a woman's anger — about how some people settle for this and some for that, but as for me, I've got to get out of here." Although Rose is singing about other things, she plays out her desire for the plaque and money. The music and lyrics create an affecting intensity.

After eight songs were completed, Styne asked Sondheim if he'd mind performing them for Cole Porter who, a bed-ridden amputee at this point, was in extremely low spirits. Sondheim, who normally hates to "perform," even in a living-room, agreed with Ethel Merman that such a performance might cheer up the gravely ill Porter. So a date was set and after dinner, while Merman watched and listened, Cole Porter was placed as comfortably as possible in a large chair and Sondheim sang the score while Styne played on a badly tuned piano. The occasion was extraordinarily charged with emotion, and Styne struggled to retain his composure: "My piano was facing the other way and I was glad because I didn't want Cole to see the tears streaming down my face. There was a special magic to our performance, I think. We had to battle emotion and we gave more." Porter had written some of Merman's biggest hits. Now, too weak to applaud, he tapped an ashtray with a spoon to let them know he appreciated the score.

The eight songs represented all of Act I. But things were not so harmonious between playwright and director. Robbins and Laurents had different concepts of *Gypsy*, though neither knew the other's thoughts. Believing that the show was to be a panorama of vaudeville, Robbins had urged Leland Hayward to audition every vaudeville actor alive and to hire animal acts and jugglers. Both Robbins and Hayward were stunned when they read the finished script and realized that it was a musical fable, "a small story musical," reports Taylor.

There was no difference of opinion about the show as far as Laurents, Styne, and Sondheim were concerned. "We never had a bad week," reminisced Sondheim. "We never had, I would say, maybe even a bad day. I can't speak for Arthur's own internal problems when he was working the book out, but I don't remember his groaning a lot. It just went right on schedule. It was one of those miracles, and I think it shows. The show has a feeling of spontaneity."

The entire score was completed in about five weeks and the fact that it was a star vehicle gave Laurents a big advantage: "I felt that Merman had a quality — with all that brassiness, a quality of naïveté, innocence. That helped me to write this woman who *really* didn't know what a monster she was. To help Ethel, I would write stage directions: 'slower,' 'faster,' 'louder,' 'softer.' You know, that's the way she acted."

During the writing of the libretto, Laurents was pleased that Robbins did not see the script and lyrics. However, this did have one costly effect: because Robbins believed he was about to do a great panorama of a show about vaudeville and burlesque, he was auditioning and casting the wrong sort of performers. On January 20, 1959, a multitude of strippers crowded the Imperial Theatre on West 45th Street in the hopes of being selected for ten roles: four for strippers and six for show-girls. Press agents remarked that there hadn't been a Broadway call for strippers since the Ziegfeld Follies.

And the assortment was a voyeur's delight as the women came from all over the Eastern Seaboard, night clubs, burlesque houses, assorted joints and dives. Some of the hopefuls were already employed and some had apparently come out of retirement in order to disrobe in a legitimate theatre. Some brought their own musicians; some brought even their own burlesque partners. Some, like Maria Karnilova, had had varied backgrounds — beginning, perhaps, in children's ballet and extending into show dancing. For three hours they shook, rolled, bumped, and jumped about. Veteran Faith Dane showed up with a bugle which she blew while undulating. According to Hollis Alpert, this inspired the number "You Gotta Have a Gimmick" which worked her into a trio of exotics: one wore flapping butterfly wings, one was electrified with lights on her costume, and Dane blew a trumpet while bumping and grinding. This burlesque scene was at Robbins's insistence because the director wanted to emphasize Gypsy Rose Lee's vocation.

Robbins did not realize as yet that he was going to be dealing with an intimate drama about three people. But Laurents never discussed this point with him because he didn't want to: "I knew what I wanted to do and the only person I collaborated with was Steve. He collaborated in his own way with Jule. The three of us would meet and play songs and we had only one disagreement. They thought 'You'll Never Get Away from Me' would be a hit and I didn't and I still don't like it. I don't think it works." This song lacked the wildness of Rose and did not seem to him to be on a par with the rest of the score.

However, as rosy as this picture sounds about the way in which the words and music came about, it should be borne in mind that the rehearsal period did entail revisions, cuts, and tightening up. No musical ever reaches its opening night on Broadway intact from first read-through to première. Directors don't always see eye-to-eye with composers or actors; playwrights discover flaws they hadn't noticed before in the scripts; designers find out that a show's focus has changed; and so on. *Gypsy* was essentially spared the kind of chaos that often bedevils a production, because it had a strong book and because its music and lyrics were set in their main patterns by the three major collaborators before the first rehearsal period.

Rehearsals

THE MAJOR CASTING PROBLEM was finding a leading man for Ethel Merman. Laurents, Robbins, and Sondheim considered Robert Wright, Gary Merrill, Edmond O'Brien, and Jack Carson, and auditioned many actors — including Victor Jory, Robert Alda, Wendell Corey, and Lew Parker — but were not truly keen on any of them, according to Merman. But when watching a segment of *Playhouse 90*, they spotted someone whom they felt had the right qualities for Herbie. This man was a Philadelphian who had studied at Carnegie Tech's drama school, then understudied Doc in *Mister Roberts* on that play's national tour. He had appeared in Equity Library productions of *Saint Joan* with Kim Stanley and *Stevedore* with Rod Steiger. In 1951 he debuted on television as a photographer in *The Front Page*, and had appeared on screen in *Twelve Angry Men* and *Cry Terror*. He was Jack Klugman, and he auditioned for Herbie not once or twice, but for three weeks. Robbins sent him to David Craig for voice lessons in order that something less objectionable and grating would emerge from his larynx when he tried to sing. "Small World," the song he had to deliver, sometimes in duet with Merman, was enough to tax a professional singer, let alone Klugman who had never been in a musical and who lacked any confidence in his own singing ability. He was an actor, not a singer, but Robbins, Merman, Sondheim, and Hayward thought him perfect for the role, except for his singing. Yet, they were also convinced that Styne would not approve of him.

Styne usually turned a singer's audition into an ordeal. His biographer notes that Styne usually asked a singer to go higher and higher, simply to determine his or her range. "But his presence alone, backed by a half century of experience, was an obstacle. Singers had been known to sweat and freeze when he stood with an ear cocked."

Styne arrived late for Klugman's final audition at the Amsterdam Theatre at Forty-second Street and Seventh Avenue. The nervous actor managed to do an excellent reading, and then tried "Small World." He had already forewarned that if Merman were to do her usual razzle-dazzle belting, he would walk straight out. But Merman, who thought him perfect for the role, encouraged him. "Come on, Jack. I know you can cut it." Anxious to let him show to his best advantage, she tried bottling up her own voice, but she sang so low that her own voice cracked. Klugman was so moved by her loving concern that he picked up and sang the second chorus like he'd never sung before. It was not Pinza or Lanza, but it sounded very much like a genuine, straight-talking man in Rose's life. Yet, Klugman did not bother to wait for reaction. He left the theatre in self-disgust.

Taylor relates that Robbins said, "Jule, there's only one problem. This man can't sing." To his surprise, Styne grinned and replied, "So what . . . He's got a lousy voice but he sounds real. That's all that counts, isn't it?".

So Klugman had the role, and an important casting problem was over. However, Laurents was particular about casting his *Gypsy*. In a letter he sent to Hayward just before writing the second act of his libretto, he declared that it was absolutely imperative that the role be played by a genuine actress, for as the play proceeded, the part grew in size and emotional range. From an insecure and rather insignificant supporting player, she changed and developed into a sophisticated, assured young woman. Only an actress could make these transitions, and anyone less would leave Merman to fend for herself — certainly something she was quite capable of doing anyway, but certainly something that would create a sense of organic failure in the play. To Laurents, all the women auditioned were a waste of time because they were basically singers or dancers rather than actresses. In his mind, ideal casting for the role would have been Anne Bancroft — the Bancroft of chic sophistication in some of her B-movies, or the gutsy ingénue of *Seesaw* — but she was unavailable. The name of Carol Lawrence was put forward for awhile, but she, too, proved to be unavailable. Finally, Sandra Church was auditioned and approved. A San Franciscan who, at the age of five, had moved with her mother to Los Angeles where she attended convent school and then studied drama and allied arts, she had sent her photograph to Joshua Logan who tested her and awarded her the part of Madge for the national tour of *Picnic*. A red-haired beauty, she then studied for four years at the Actors Studio with Lee Strasberg.

The final cast included Lane Bradbury as June and Mort Marshall as Mr. Goldstone. Born and educated in Atlanta, Bradbury, like Church, was a member of the Actors Studio. She left the cast of Archibald MacLeish's *J.B.* (in which she had made her Broadway début) in order to be in *Gypsy*. Marshall, a veteran of over two hundred television appearances (on such programs as *Kraft, Omnibus,* and *Ed Sullivan*), specialized in comedy roles. His last four Broadway shows had played a total of only seven performances, so he was more than ready and due for a hit. Maria Karnilova, Faith Dane, and Chotzi Foley were the tough strippers, Tessie Tura, Mazeppa, and Electra.

Rehearsals began on February 11, 1959. The renowned Jo Mielziner was commissioned to do the settings and lighting, with Raoul Pène du Bois responsible for the costumes. About four months earlier, Leland Hayward had approached Cecil Beaton to design the sets, but Beaton, the most rarefied of Edwardian stylists, did not like Gypsy Rose Lee's book and did not feel that the striptease world was his idiom. As it turned out, Mielziner was the better choice. Born in Paris in 1901, he had received his early education in France. In 1907 he was sent to a boarding school in England and then to New York two years later. He came from cultured stock: his father was a noted portrait painter, his mother a fashion and theatre correspondent for *Vogue*. His ancestors included two prominent nineteenth-century theatre figures, Charlotte Cushman and Dan McGinnis. In 1916 Mielziner was offered a scholarship at the Pennsylvania Academy of Fine Arts, but acting upon the advice of friends and his own parents, he decided to leave school and study painting full time. After brief service in the Marines, he returned to Pennsylvania and in 1920 and 1922 won Cresson Traveling Scholarships, which he used to study contemporary theatre in Europe. His first professional experience came in 1921 when he joined Jessie Bonstelle's stock company in Detroit as actor, designer, and stage manager. He was not keen on being an actor, but his brother Kenneth, a professional actor who appeared under the name of Kenneth McKenna, advised him to play small parts in order to see plays from an actor's point of view. In 1923 he made his New York début as a bit player and assistant stage manager for the soon-to-be-famous Theatre Guild, where he worked under the supervision of Lee Simonson, an expert designer who was very conscious of lighting techniques. Mielziner's career as designer really began in the 1924–25 season when the Guild commissioned him to do Molnar's *The Guardsman* for Alfred Lunt and Lynn Fontanne.

Mielziner made the usual mistakes of a young designer. He mistook means for ends, looked upon the theatre merely as a way of earning a living rather than as a living art, and remained blind to the true values of theatre. "I confess my unbounded delight in my early days at seeing my settings revealed by glamorous stage lighting after they were completed at dress-rehearsal time. I almost resented the prospect of actors standing between my picture and the admiring audience!" Despite the revolutionary influence of Robert Edmond Jones, who simplified design to its essentials so that every line counted in terms of theatrical effect, American stage design at this point was still a literal attempt at realism — sometimes skillful, sometimes plain, occasionally tawdry or uninteresting. Mielziner, who first saw Jones's work in 1915, gradually absorbed the master's lessons and discovered that lighting was as important a part of design as décor. He also learned that it was possible to suggest more truth by less explicit detail, at least in the sense of pictorial realism. "The good theatre artist is never 'actual.' He omits the nonessentials, condenses the essentials, accents the details that are the most revealing. He depicts only that part of the truth which he deems necessary to the course of the story."

Mielziner learned avidly from Jones, Simonson, and Joseph Urban, and his own designs became signal ones. For *The Glass Menagerie* (1945), he used translucent and transparent scenic interior walls as a true reflection of Tennessee Williams's interest in the inner man. For *Finian's Rainbow* (1947), he created the atmosphere of a languid, crumbling Southern mansion by painting effects with translucent aniline on seamless, specially treated muslin. In *A Streetcar Named*

Desire (1947), he made dramatic use of poetic lighting, and the set had a brooding atmosphere even as it resembled an impressionistic x-ray of a tenement. Whether he worked in straight dramas or on Broadway musicals, the Mielziner signature was unmistakable. *Guys and Dolls* (1950) created a zany world but heightened by garish colours. *The Innocents* (1951) was moody, shadowy, ghostly. *The King and I* (1951) used memories of his visit to Bangkok rather than museum accuracy for the Orientalia. *Can-Can* (1953) imitated the vital colour contrasts of Toulouse-Lautrec, as hot, flaming yellows and oranges contrasted with luminous greens.

Mielziner's numerous awards — including five Donaldson Awards, three Tonys, and numerous Variety Poll citations — had added much lustre to his career. And *Gypsy* should have been a big, colourful exercise for him with its range of vaudeville and burlesque haunts and sense of restless movement. But like all musicals, *Gypsy* was growing and changing in production, and the director's requirements and musical staging altered in the rehearsal process. The results, under the circumstances, did not satisfy his own high standards, but they were striking all the same, revealing extensive scene-painting, many flats, and clever lighting. The designs included a tacky vaudeville theatre; an airy restaurant with a few lanterns and curtains and large stencilled words in the free space; dingy backstage corridors and prop rooms; Gypsy's dressing room replete with nude female statue decorated with G-string and jewels; and, climactically, a bare stage for "Rose's Turn," with only a large, plain backdrop, theatre sandbag, and rigging. The visual effect of the setting and lighting for "Rose's Turn" was an emblematic summary of the character's isolation and desperation. This dramatic idiom stood in startling contrast to the bright pastel corniness of the second-rate vaudeville routines for the children or the garish vulgarity of the Christmas at Minsky's spectacle.

Mielziner had a good costume designer in Raoul Pène du Bois whose work was at once witty and emblematic. A native New Yorker, born on Staten Island in 1914, du Bois was a true eccentric. Descended from New Orleans stock, he had colourful roots. At the turn of the century, his grandfather, Henri Pène Du Bois, wrote on literature

and drama in Paris for an American newspaper chain. An uncle was a noted portrait painter; a cousin, William, was a famed author and illustrator of prize-winning children's books. At thirteen, Raoul was himself distinguished. As a young boy he had seen Hippodrome spectacles and had been terrified by the colours on stage. This led to an important insight: colour was something to be used gently, not splashed about. He lost his father early in boyhood, but this did not stifle his self-confidence or independence. Assured of his own artistic talent, he turned down an art scholarship at sixteen because he did not think he required one after selling a design for the Garrick Gaieties. Quickly, however, he had to turn to lesser jobs, such as dressing windows at $35 a week. He quit after the second week and tried stencilling wallpaper. Fortunately, he was able to sell a couple of sketches of Radio City Music Hall, which caught the eye of director Vincente Minnelli who was in charge of the shows, and du Bois was given a job at $100 a month. He quit in a few weeks because someone criticized his work. Lee Simonson came to his rescue after seeing some of his scenic drawings. Simonson encouraged him to contact professionals, but du Bois experienced no luck. Eventually, he had a sketch accepted by *Vogue*, then several others by *Harper's Bazaar*. In 1934 he was taken to John M. Anderson by Ted Weidhaus, the mechanical wizard who had constructed the amazing contour curtain at Radio City Music Hall. Anderson was directing the Shubert Ziegfeld Follies. According to a *New York Times* story which ran on 8 Sept. 1940, the eccentric Englishman regarded the trembling youth fiercely and announced: "You look like a poor, famished faun! You can't have eaten in months. I shall call you 'One More Spring.'"
The odd nickname stuck — even into his Broadway career where at twenty-six he had the distinction of being the most *recherché* scene designer.

Pène du Bois's flourishing Broadway career began in 1934, when he was hired by Anderson to do costumes for the mimes in *Thumbs Up*, a twenty-week disappointment. Then he became a Billy Rose ward, whipping up a collection of clown uniforms with tinsel and spangles for *Jumbo* (1935), starring Jimmy Durante. Against Albert Johnson's vermilion sets, the costumes were a colourful riot. Billy

Rose's showmanship provoked du Bois's own flamboyance. Commissioned by Rose to design a rodeo just outside Fort Worth in 1936, he stepped off a plane in Texas, dressed in green Tyrolean costume with short leather knee-pants, embroidered stockings, and the word *Prosit* embroidered on his tunic. A Tyrolean cloth hat sat on his head, with a brush jutting up behind, a long cock-pheasant feather sweeping alongside, and a row of medals sewn on the crown. Texas took a little while to recover, but finally accepted him as a phenomenon to be seen rather than understood. Elliott Arnold joked that when du Bois took to wearing a belt made up of playing cards, the numerals and designs of which were heightened with imitation rubies and jades, "Cowboys were known to climb sadly on their horses and lope back to the recesses of their ranches after one look at Mr. du Bois' belt."

His show costumes could be just as eye-catching. For *A Lake Erie Aquacade* in 1940, he did Neptune-style garments with fishnet and imitation clamshells woven into jackets and tights. His sets and costumes for *Du Barry Was a Lady* (1939), which set him the challenge of designing and supervising 360 costumes in a week, represented both 18th and 20th centuries with a flamboyant elegance. For *Heaven on Earth* (1948), what Gerald Bordman calls "a dim-witted, banal, and unmelodic affair that ran 12 performances," he did a magnificent re-creation of Central Park and a comic, push-button-bedevilled "Hutton Home of Tomorrow." Acclaim for *Du Barry* and other shows — *Panama Hattie* (1940), *Carmen Jones* (1943), *Call Me Madam* (1950), *Wonderful Town* (1953), and *The Music Man* (1957) — brought him national fame. He won Donaldson and Tony awards for *Wonderful Town*, and three Oscar nominations for his costume designs for *Lady in the Dark* (1943), *Frenchman's Creek* (1944), and *Kitty* (1945).

As a designer, he refused to allow costumes to be unobtrusive. "Nothing should be done for beauty, just for beauty," he told the *World-Telegram*. "Costumes should be part of the scene, exaggeration and suggestion more than anything else, I should say. It's hell on the people who have to wear them, I'll admit, but I'm opposed to the school of thought that feels the set and costumes should be unobtrusive and retiring." He did not regard costumes and sets as background, and he fought hard for what he wanted in a show. He strongly believed that the theatre should produce "a sort of unreal brilliance," as opposed to realism. (The movies did realism a lot better.) The theatre was quite "unreal" and should stay that way. "I approve of footlights, which is supposed to be old-fashioned. It [sic] lights persons and costumes and sets from the bottom, which is thoroughly unreal."

Gypsy gave him another wonderful opportunity to indulge some of his old tricks of "unreal brilliance," for he could now go for carnival cheapness in the vaudeville and burlesque scenes, and still have street clothes that would suit the personality of the rest of the show. The tawdry could be set against the commonplace, and lighting would heighten the effects. The production developed a running-joke about Rose's stinginess through fabric and cut. But the joke was not overblown and it issued directly out of Laurents's script. Without making it too obvious, the production had blankets lying around in one scene. Then two scenes later, the audience would see Rose and her daughters in wild coats. This bafflingly strange look would suddenly prompt the audience into recognizing that the material for the coats had come from the hotel blankets that Rose had obviously stolen. But the pause between the first gasp of surprise and the payoff guffaw signified that the joke worked subtly and was not simply a bald sight-gag. Stephen Sondheim claims that the audience reaction built cumulatively: "The scene started, and it was 'What's wrong with this picture?' And then somebody in the audience would start to laugh, and the other people would whisper, and then soon the whole audience would go. It was *never* pointed out. It was just a subtlety, a through-line."

The costumes met every demand of the show. They were dramatically expressive for Mama Rose, emblematic of Baby June's juvenile innocence, and Herbie's plain honesty, satiric for the three exotic strippers, and mammothly vulgar for the large production number with the Christmas and Stars and Stripes motifs. Soft, sometimes furry, textures were exploited for June; beiges and tans for the earnest, anxious Herbie; and reds, whites, and blues for the big production number that glittered with lavish bad taste. Mama Rose's costumes were the central focus because they reflected her adult-child dichotomy in the oversize bow and the bouclé suits.

One of the problems for the show was the opening. How was the audience to be involved almost immediately? Laurents wanted to give Ethel Merman a star entrance because she had to practically start the show. He did not feel that she could sing at that point, so the question became how to introduce her theatrically and really startle the audience. His solution, according to Otis Guernsey, was to make her come down the auditorium aisle, thereby illustrating her disruptiveness in two senses: she would disrupt the scene on the main stage, as well as the audience's composure in the auditorium.

But this opening was not the very first image of the show. Initially, the play began with a rehearsal scene in a vaudeville house, and the first thing the audience would see was a woman playing a scene. There was a painted flat of a fireplace and a girl in a sailor middy blouse. The first words spoken were a terrible monologue that set the mother-daughter theme, for the woman would reveal to the girl that she was not her sister but her mother. This ended in a blackout, whereupon stage-hands came on to remove the painted flat and to make room for Uncle Jocko and the Kiddie show. The audience was supposed to realize at this point that the setting was a vaudeville house in which had just been presented a dramatic scene prior to a musical number. The original opening was weirdly comic and very appropriate to the form of old-style entertainment, but the elaborateness increased the length of Gypsy, and it was cut during the Philadelphia run.

Originally, too, "Let Me Entertain You" was meant "to show up in each of the vaudeville acts but with different titles." But then Sondheim decided it would be better to use the same title all the time so that the audience would have some fun wondering where it had heard that title before. The inherent joke, of course, was that Rose would not write new lyrics or pay for them.

Gypsy gambled on a bold device of having the main character come right out and reveal herself to the audience, not so much through action as through asides or sung monologues. Merman, much respected and feared by her colleagues, behaved beautifully throughout rehearsals, never pulling rank, always seeking to draw the best out of her fellow-players. She did insist on having Lew Kesler as her rehearsal pianist because he had worked with her off and on since 1935, rehearsing her for shows and also playing in the pit during the run. A friend of hers, his most recent musical association with her had been on *Happy Hunting*, and there was no greater accompanist for her. She was certainly not willing to "break in" a new man when Kesler knew every breath she took when working. Jule Styne, who had won his bid to have Milton Rosenstock conduct the show (he had conducted practically everything Styne had written for the theatre), was not averse to yielding to Merman's desire. Everybody on the production team knew that Merman was anxious to prove that she was more than a singer or comedienne. She was eagerly attempting to widen her acting range. She did not mind that seven of her eight songs were intentionally designed to kill any applause that threatened to break or dilute a scene's specific mood. She later claimed to be all for strengthening the production's impact, and liked the fact that Styne's numbers were "dramatic songs with dimension" and that Styne was "reaching out, stretching himself" just as she was. Only one thing bothered her: she did not have a number that would give the driving Rose applause for herself. "Some People," her first number, was a bit of a show-off piece for the character, and Merman (perhaps subconsciously) had tried to make it a personal triumph and performed it a little outside the unpleasant character she was portraying. As Sondheim recalls, "No matter how well and how intensely she sang it, she *always* snapped her fingers during the number. In my opinion it was because she wanted the audience to know, 'Look, you are going on a trip tonight with a very unpleasant woman. Remember this is Ethel, o.k.?" Sondheim gave her a note on this a couple of times, and although she was surprised to hear about her finger-snapping mannerism, she never ever broke the habit. But "she played the rest of the show uncompromisingly."

Laurents had devised a cute but chilling third scene. The two sisters were atop a flat and spying on their mother who was in the process of flirting with Herbie and conning him into handling her act. The girls were shown to be wise but already jaded. They knew exactly what was transpiring and they sang something called "Mama's Talking Soft." The idea of the song was that Rose used disarmingly deceitful means to take over a situation or a person. Then Rose and Herbie sang "Small World," and then the two songs went together charmingly in counterpoint. Unfortunately, Karen Moore (who played young Louise) suffered from acute acrophobia and when she was twelve or fifteen feet in the air, her resolve to be a good little brave actress broke down and she cried hysterically. Nobody had the nerve or cruelty to coax her into trying again. The producers could have fired her, but Sondheim and Styne decided it was more humane to cut the song.

Two other songs from the original score were also cut. One had been for Merman, and the other for Klugman, and they both happened and disappeared during the Philadelphia try-out. In fact, one lasted but a single performance, and the other never really got tried out in actual production. Merman's number was an attempt to open Act II. It was a comic song entitled "Smile, Girls," in which Rose was coaching the Toreadorables on how to smile. The situation was simple: after rehearsing a terrible tango, the girls sat around Rose in a semi-circle and she advised them: "Smile, girls, / And you'll lay 'em in the aisle, girls. / When you smile, girls, / You don't need a plot." Rose obviously drew upon her worldly wise experience, audacity, deviousness, and dissimulation in order to inject vitality and courage into the act. It was a comic song, but so very characteristic of Rose's fortitude and resourcefulness as it urged the girls to flaunt their youth, juvenile pulchritude, and simulated sophistication before men in order to drive them crazy.

Klugman's song was a solo that Styne and Sondheim composed to be performed when Rose leaves a restaurant after stealing the silverware. When a waitress appeared and asked, "Where is that nice lady?" he was to sing "Nice She Ain't." When he first heard the number, Klugman was thrilled, but with the New York opening only a week away, he asked for time to think about it overnight. Unfortunately, he had a terrible nightmare of 1800 people witnessing his singing off-key, so the next day, according to Zadan, he walked over to Styne and said, "Take the song and shove it up your ass!"

Apart from these cuts and a revision of "Shut Up and Dance" (which became "All I Need Is the Girl"), the score and lyrics shaped up smoothly. Merman immersed herself thoroughly in rehearsals, not showing that she minded the romantic affair off-stage between Sandra Church and Jule Styne. "Merman was marvelous in rehearsal," Laurents claims. "She was very professional and very willing. You couldn't have asked for any star to act better than she did." But she did balk once and once refused to learn a new lyric. When Laurents added the line "I did it for me" to her dialogue in the last scene, Merman did not want to say it. However, she relented upon seeing the necessity for having Rose face herself and admit some culpability and vulnerability. For all Rose's toughness, she is supposed to be revealed in the moment as a little girl whose elder daughter now becomes her emotional support.

Merman, however, refused to yield on a second matter. This almost ended her amiable relationship with Sondheim, but she had always insisted that she would accept any changes in a show up until a week before the opening. Thereafter, she would utterly refuse to alter a single word, gesture, or move. Two weeks before the opening, Sondheim felt that "Some People" needed a verse to bring the song down a pitch or two. The cue-in was clumsy and required the new verse. Merman, however, felt that it was too angry and refused to learn it. Sondheim appealed to the Dramatists Guild but was told that the personal factor involved in his case superseded his legal rights. After all, the star was Merman — who had refused to accept Irving Berlin's revised lyric for a song in *Call Me Madam* because she considered the show frozen a week before the opening. If the great Berlin could not prevail, then surely Sondheim should forget his cause.

Other than these two contretemps, Merman was the very picture of co-operation. She never sought to alter the script or lyrics, though she did have one nagging concern. She felt something lacking in her playing of Rose or, perhaps, something lacking for Rose's sake. Rose's final song came at the very end of the piece, after Gypsy's first big smash as an ecdysiast, so the moment had to be big theatrically, dramatically, and musically in order to top Gypsy's striptease number. Sondheim insisted that the moment of Rose's nervous breakdown should not have applause because this made no sense in terms of dramatic or psychological truth. Originally, "Rose's Turn" was designed by Robbins as a ballet, with the character seeing her past in a visual reprise with nightmare figures. The first version of the number was rejected by Robbins because it was not big enough for Rose's climactic moment. "The material has to be bigger," he complained. "It isn't now. She has to sing for at least five minutes, solid. I'm not going to do it with staging or tricks." "Rose's Turn" as a ballet was out of sorts with the rest of the show. "It was much too pretentious and entirely wrong," says Sondheim. "So it devolved on us — Jule and me — to try to carry out Arthur's idea of climaxing the show this way, but with no help from anything except the singer herself." Styne and Sondheim both knew that "Rose's Turn" would have to be a summary of what the character was all about. What complicated the creation of suitable music and lyrics for it was that the number came after a sample of Gypsy Rose Lee's new life on the Minsky circuit. Styne wanted to give Merman something huge, a powerful musical review of her life at a point when she realized that her daughters did not need her anymore. She had to be determined to force Gypsy to understand what Rose had contributed to their lives and careers. "It was her turn to tell everyone that they were what she'd made them. It's rather easy to say in words but to say it musically is more difficult." Sondheim knew that to just have Rose come out and sing thirty-two bars at the point, even twice, would not achieve the desired effect. He forced Styne not to put an ending on the number, but to "have it fade out with high scratchy violin sounds with those two last chords when she's screaming — not singing, but screaming — 'For me, for me, for me!' " Sondheim saw the scene as an arc which traced the beginning of Rose's breakdown to her capitulation in the three-page scene and on to the final curtain. He wanted a chillingly quiet finish, with Louise emerging from the wings to applaud Rose and lead her off as a mother would a daughter.

Merman was herself dissatisfied. Although very impressed with the score on the whole, she wanted a show-stopper. She wanted a blazing ending, especially as Gypsy was upstage while Rose was having her breakdown. Merman said, "Look, I have to have a finish for this. I've worked too hard. I demand I have a finish — 'for me, for me, for MEEEE!' Vooooom! Then let her [Louise] come in."

The deciding factor was a tryout performance in Philadelphia which Oscar Hammerstein attended. Laurents and Sondheim invited him for a drink afterwards and coaxed a reaction out of him. "I thought there were three major problems," Hammerstein began. "The first one is the doorknob in the kitchen set keeps falling off every time anyone comes in. It's very distracting." Laurents and Sondheim were secretly relieved at this criticism, for it was really a minor one. " 'You'll Never Get Away from Me' ought to end that scene," Hammerstein continued. The song was in the middle of the scene, and Hammerstein commented: "Generally it's good to end a scene with a song." This made good sense for a show that demanded concentration on the unfolding drama of characters. Finally, Hammerstein said: "And you must give Ethel Merman an ending on 'Rose's Turn.' " Sondheim started to bristle and asked, "Why?" "Because the audience is so anxious to applaud her that they are not listening to the scene that follows. Since the scene that follows is what the entire play is about, if you want them to listen, you must let them release themselves." Hammerstein acknowledged that this was dishonest and a ruse, but he pleaded with Laurents and Sondheim "to put a big ending on that number" if they wanted the rest of the play to work. The only other option, he claimed, was to bring the curtain down right there. "You have to choose one of those two things."

Laurents and Sondheim considered the matter and then concocted "an emotionally fake-ending on that song." Rose now screamed away and suddenly hit her big cadence, letting the audience think that they were in a musical and thus giving them the opportunity to applaud and cry out and relieve their emotions before settling down for the final scene.

The nightmare quality that Robbins wanted required what Sondheim calls "a kind of interrupted consciousness technique." Instead of a visual reprise of Rose's life — as Robbins's ballet was going to be — the moment became variations of songs heard before in a sort of "nightmare version." Sondheim: "There are some melodic variations with dissonant accompaniments and some lyrical variations, and they play off all that you've heard and seen all evening, which gives the number a kaleidoscopic feel."

Trusting very much in Jerome Robbins's expertise, Merman learned her soliloquy by following behind him as he walked through the number. She called him "Teacher," and he was one of her favourite directors — along with Joshua Logan and George Abbott — so she relied on him to teach her how to move and gesticulate for her most demanding and testing role. Robbins taught her how to use stillness and economy of gesture for dramatic effect, and Merman says that she felt very strongly that she had "never been presented to better advantage" in any other musical.

The waiver problem with June Havoc continued. She had not yet signed a release form and kept insisting on alterations to the script. She wanted Baby June to be an audience charmer and for Rose and Louise to be less sensitive. Laurents first tried to appease her, but when her demands grew damaging to his own vision of the characters, he refused to make any further alterations. She wanted June to be only eleven at the end of Act I when she elopes with her teenage lover. This was clearly inaccurate historically and very damaging to Rose's character for now the mother would appear to be a thorough monster and quite beyond horror in musical theatre. Havoc threatened an injunction to stop rehearsals of a show that the producers did not legally own. But then David Merrick came up with a bright idea. He was a lawyer himself and well versed in libel laws. He decided to change the name of the character from Baby June to Baby Claire. Then he billed the show as a musical fable and vowed to keep Havoc so tied up with lawyers that she'd be powerless herself to stop the show. According to Preminger, Merrick was proving to be a slicker version of Mike Todd — the sort of man that Gypsy Rose Lee had so loved.

Three-quarters of the way into rehearsal, Laurents and Robbins both recognized that the play was far too long — by perhaps as much as forty-five minutes. Robbins had devised an elaborate burlesque show which actually distracted the audience's attention from Gypsy and Mama Rose. In the second act, Laurents had created a marvellous moment when Louise (once a girl who wore pants and not skirts) put on makeup and transformed herself into Gypsy Rose Lee. There followed a scene with Herbie, then her first big strip, then a floral tribute from Rose which she had stolen from somewhere. All this was done in sequence and not as a montage of effects. We saw Louise's vital transformation from girl to confident woman. We saw the backstage drama when Rose demanded top billing for her daughter. But it was all too drawn out. Styne offered a solution, which was to combine the backstage scenes before and after the strip. Gypsy would go off-stage to dress, Rose and Herbie would have their scene with his finally leaving her. Then Gypsy would enter in her strip costume. All this would build dramatically to the strip, which would now become a montage of strips to suggest a passage of time and carry us to the final scenes. Acting upon Styne's advice, Laurents marked twenty minutes of cuts in his script. Robbins heard about this and asked when Laurents was going to make the cuts. "When you cut twenty minutes from those kiddie numbers," shot back Laurents. Robbins had no leverage: "Okay, you take your cuts and I'll take mine."

Rumblings and grumblings of discontent grew. Tempers flared. Nerves were on edge. Robbins was dissatisfied with the show and his own limited impact on it. He would always say to Laurents, "It's your show, it's a book show." Clearly, the director did not enjoy the sort of creative power he had wielded in *West Side Story*, where he had been able to conceive, choreograph, and direct very much on his own terms. *Gypsy* severely restricted his contribution.

For his part, David Merrick also acted strangely on occasion. According to Guernsey, he kept muttering, "My God, this show is terrible." (Later he would claim that he said this merely to stop the cast and crew from getting smug.) He also remarked three times, "I want to get rid of the show." Jack Klugman verifies the stories about Merrick. When Klugman wanted to invest in *Gypsy*, Merrick tried to dissuade him, "You don't want to invest in this. It's going to be a bomb. If you want to invest in a musical, invest in *Destry*." Hayward and Styne, who were present with Klugman at the Variety Club, immediately pulled out their cheque-books and said, "How much would you take to get out of this show?" Merrick immediately shut up.

As the Philadelphia opening drew nearer, Styne completed the overture and rehearsed the music with orchestra leader Milton Rosenstock in Philadelphia's Masonic Temple. Theodore Taylor notes that it went badly, and nobody was sure how to end the piece — until Styne noticed that the second trumpet of the three in the orchestra was the strongest and best. Styne suddenly yelled from the piano, "We got to make it alive!" Then he ran over to the second trumpet and told him how to play the notes. The next afternoon in the theatre, where Laurents, Robbins, Hayward, Merrick, and Sondheim were in attendance, Rosenstock led the orchestra through the entire overture to a dead silence. Rosenstock turned around to see the high command staring at Styne. "Robbins's thumb was pointed down." Styne conferred briefly with his colleagues and then approached the orchestra pit:

"What's wrong?" Milton asked.
"They don't want it."
"They're crazy. . . What *do* they want?"
"Play a chorus of this, play a chorus of that. The same old shit. Christ, I knew it." [Styne was exasperated.]

Robbins came down the aisle with a killingly cold look. Rosenstock exclaimed: "Jerry, you're wrong, you're dead wrong." He implored the stubborn director to try the overture for one performance. Robbins agreed to a preview trial, but delivered an ultimatum: "If it doesn't go, we do the choruses." Styne was furious. "Not okay with me. . . . We open with this goddamn overture. I'll not cut one minute of it." Then Styne resorted to his own stratagem. Just before the first preview curtain at the Shubert, he went over to the second trumpet, Dick Perry, and said, "When we come to that part with your high E-flat screams, I want you to stand up and blow the ceiling off."

A beleaguered Rosenstock began the overture, and when Perry

arose and started riffing and blowing, he was hardly past three bars when the audience applauded and bravoed. They were still cheering when Rosenstock hit the cue for Merman's entrance.

At intermission when Rosenstock hugged Styne backstage, Robbins was still disconcerted: "I still don't like it." Styne shrugged; there was nothing more he could or would do about the matter.

However, the overall reaction to the show was tame. The Philadelphia *Inquirer* complained that *Gypsy* was "unconscionably long" and that while there was "plenty of situation humor," one felt "that the fields of burlesque and vaudeville should invoke a little more of the 'gag' type of humor." Its critic found that, though the story kept her from blossoming fully until late in the evening, Sandra Church was winsome as Louise, and added nice words about others in the cast — particularly Carole D'Andrea as June, Jack Klugman, and the burlesque queens (Karnilova, Dane, and Foley). Mielziner's sets were praised but, as expected, it was Merman who dominated the primarily mixed reviews. Taylor reports that only the notice in the *Philadelphia Bulletin* was thoroughly positive: "There is only one reaction to *Gypsy* and that is unconditional surrender. Jule Styne has written the most serious score of his career."

Merman's reviews were glorious. The Philadelphia *Daily News* maintained that the "almost Dostoevskian" length of the show was "no grind" with Merman as the mom:

> Never the one to approach a characterization half-heartedly, Miss Merman gives us a portrait of the stage mother that should serve as a standard for all future studies of this grasping fiercely aggressive, self-anointed type. . . . The star does the lion's share of the vocalizing, holding those top tones as is her vaunted custom.

Gypsy Rose Lee visited Merman backstage and confessed that the star had made her cry. Merman was pleased to hear this because this meant that her interpretation was validated. Merman had not played the part as if Rose were merely selfish and self-centered; rather, she had interpreted Rose as someone who wanted everything for her girls. Merman took as her cue the lines in "Rose's Turn," "I dreamed it for you, June. / It wasn't for me, Herbie." Only after her daughters had shown that they were independent of her did she eventually take her turn. Merman herself says that "Mamma Rose sacrificed her whole life, gave up the love of her life for Louise and June. That's why when I played her, I got sympathy. People cried."

But because of her extraordinary efforts, the show was exhausting for her. Even at intermission Merman was tired and had to hold her head in her hands as she bent over in a chair in her dressing room. One night, as the second-half buzzer sounded, she remarked to Styne who frequently visited her, "Hey, I want to tell you something. This is a hard show to do every night."

According to Taylor, one of the eminent visitors to the show was June Havoc, who was still a thorn in the sides of the producers. The actors were experiencing difficulty adjusting to the name change from "June" to "Claire," or some hybrid. Havoc was not amused. Whatever its manifestation, the name-change meant that she was not really in the show at all as a character. She signed the long-awaited release and her true first name returned to the script.

There were now about five weeks to go till the New York performances, and Laurents and Robbins still quarrelled over the form and content of the show. The musical was still a bit long, as Robbins kept attempting to make it more of a dancing show. At the end of the original version of Scene 6 with the "Mr. Goldstone, I Love You" number, the mood is festive and not a little silly. The song itself has a one-joke idea as the lyric repeats the same idea of bribery over and over, but everybody in the room is happy. Then the audience suddenly notices that Louise is missing. The song comes to a freezing stop, the lights switch, and then in another room we see Louise, all alone with her animals. This is when she sings "Little Lamb." The plaintive moment also offers respite from Mama Rose's relentlessly driving power. Robbins, however, was convinced that this staging would not work, and managed to have his way with re-staging the scene. He divided the scene and the songs, and ended up winning applause for "Mr. Goldstone." Guernsey notes that "Little Lamb" was not the kind of tune to win a hand, and Robbins appeared to have made his point that the new arrangement, with Louise's senti-mental song separated from the raucously festive "Mr. Goldstone" one, preserved the rhythm of the scene without losing any values.

Robbins, however, did not leave well enough alone. Still dissatis-fied with the orchestrations and overture, he abruptly cut "Little Lamb" from the show without consulting either Styne or Laurents. When Styne heard of the cut, he asked Robbins to re-insert the song into the show. Robbins refused, so Styne walked up to the stage and announced: "Mr. Robbins, I have notified my lawyers in New York that I'm withdrawing the entire score unless 'Little Lamb' is put back in tonight." Styne's cold dignity, poise, and ultimatum unnerved the normally undeterred Robbins, who promptly gave in and restored the song.

Gypsy moved out of Philadelphia in mid-May to begin previews in New York prior to the May 21 première. Everybody, except Robbins, was satisfied in the main with the show which, at last, was "frozen" — in other words, left blessedly free from any more tampering or snipping. But there was a new problem all of a sudden.

At the Winter Garden the orchestra was practically buried in the pit, hence producing a not very impressive sound. Styne requested special platforms from which the musicians could produce tones that would not sound submerged. But two previews went by without the requested platforms. At about three o'clock in the afternoon of the official opening, Styne walked in and noticed the orchestra still very much in the pit. He stomped up to Hayward: "Where are my platforms?" Hayward responded by saying that the music was loud enough. "What the hell do you know about music, Leland?" Styne thundered, making his way toward Jerome Robbins who, for some inexplicable reason, was dancing around on the bare stage with a little cap on his head. Further incensed by Robbins's apparent non-chalance, Styne grabbed him by the throat and said, "Jerry, I know you're responsible for those orchestra platforms not being here. You're destroying me. Jerry, I am going to throw you into the pit. Not only that, but when you yell, no one will hear you, just like no one will hear my music!" Robbins protested that the producers were the culprits, and added: "Oh, baby, I'll fix it." Then he tried to summon stagehands, but unfortunately they had all gone home. Hayward left next, followed by Robbins. Styne was devastated.

Suddenly, George Gilbert, a friend, showed up and suggested diplomatically that he would fetch some bar stools that would raise the musicians a foot or so. Gilbert hauled in twenty-four stools by six that evening from a friend's wholesale chair store, and later, as the theatre filled with an audience, Styne ran down to the pit and lifted the velour over the top rail.

At intermission, Robbins commented to Styne that the music was clearly audible.

"Yes, baby," Styne replied. "They're sitting a foot and a half higher, on bar stools."

Broadway Hit

THERE IS ALWAYS A BUZZ of anticipation at any première, and the opening of *Gypsy* on May 21, 1959, was no exception. Ethel Merman was, of course, a big Broadway star, and in all her press interviews had sent out clear vibrations of how optimistic and excited she was over the show which she saw as a dramatic breakthrough for herself. "You're going to see a different Merman than the one you've seen before," she announced. "I only know that I've never been presented to better advantage than in *Gypsy*. This is the peak of my career."

Gypsy Rose Lee herself saw the show in a similar light. For her, though, it was more than a peak; it was her long sought-after "moment." Nothing had worked better in her life and career than gimmicks. "That's what they bought, that's what they wanted," she had said about her audiences. She well knew that the musical was a fable — just as her own memoir had been in many respects — but this fable could be golden if the show became a hit. And with Merman in it, it could become a mega hit, as well as a vital theatrical monument to her legendary greatness as a burlesque performer.

She glowed as she walked down the aisle to her seat, escorted by her son, Erik. Wearing a long black silk and taffeta skirt belted at the waist, a white silk blouse, sable jacket, and antique diamond pendant earrings, she was stunningly elegant, and far outshone the overdressed, bejewelled society matrons who gawked and gaped at her.

While awaiting the dimming of the house-lights and the striking up of the overture, her son noticed all eyes on his mother. The real Gypsy was the most important person in the house that night, and Erik could be forgiven a little hyperbole when he later wrote: "She was the reason that everyone else was there. She *was* the show."

Any première finds cast and crew nervous — either about pleasing the audience and critics or about ensuring that their pay-cheques will continue for a decent period of time. Ethel Merman, however, was true to her reputation and form as a calm, cool professional. A few hours earlier, Benay Venuta, one of her friends and colleagues, had been a perspiring wreck, while Merman had sat at home polishing the jewelry that she was going to wear after the opening. She appeared to have no nerves, even though the opening's special guests included Richard Rodgers, Howard Lindsay, Russel Crouse, William Paley, Irene Selznick, Sam Spiegel, Mary Martin, Irving Berlin, Leonard Bernstein, Alan Jay Lerner, Joshua Logan, Truman Capote, Henry Fonda, and Dore Schary. Merman's usual attitude was that she knew all her lines, blocking, and lyrics, so why should she worry? Besides, nobody else in the theatre that night could do the job as well as she could.

The overture was stirring, right from the drum roll and trumpet flourish to the full strings and race through "Everything's Coming Up Roses," used obviously as some sort of anthem for the show. The quick tempo was good for the spirit and tenor of the work, and created an upbeat mood. As in the previews, the audience cheered at the strip music passage. There were thirty men in the orchestra and they produced a full, rich sound. Smaller instrumental groups within the orchestra were used to give authentic sounds of vaudeville and burlesque as done in the twenties. The lyrics, being in the vernacular, had a tendency to become satirical, but they also managed to be genuinely nostalgic rather than artificially worked up for effect.

Tiny lights above the stage flashed the name "Gypsy Rose Lee." Although he had been used to seeing his mother's name in lights, this spectacle gave Erik Preminger a chill. He grabbed his mother's hand and squeezed. She reciprocated, and the pair sat holding hands for much of the first act.

There seemed to be nothing superfluous about the show in this portion, especially not with Merman on stage. In the ragged audition scene for Uncle Jocko, she bolted down the auditorium aisle in order to blackmail the harried producer. As Walter Kerr described it, she lunged from the wings to straighten out a dancer's costume while the act was in progress, and when her daughters were singing, she silently mouthed their lyrics, while squinting hopefully toward the front of the house for approval. Everything she did was seemingly for the act — right from the idiot kiddie shows filled with star-spangled banners, dancing horses, and screaming newsboys to her ploy of hiding behind telephone poles while the children hitched rides, then jumping quickly into the cut-out revue-sketch car. She stole Boy Scouts for the act, slept her charges six in a room, made clothes for herself and daughters out of stolen hotel blankets (a nice costume joke by Raoul Pène du Bois), and screamingly pretended to be sexually assaulted by the manager who merely wished to collect rent. In short, said Walter Kerr, she was "a brassy, brazen witch on a mortgaged broomstick, a steamroller with cleats, the very mastodon of all stage mothers." And the audience loved her. As they also did the range of shabby, drab boarding-houses, gaudy vaudeville costumes, the twilit desert set for the car breakdown, and the moonlit alleys. While it was true that Mielziner's sets — especially for the vaudeville and burlesque houses — were cleaner than their real-life equivalents, they had enough gritty detail and closely observed texture to seem representatively realistic.

It helped that so many of the opening night audience were theatrical insiders, for in the scene between Merman and Klugman, when she was getting nowhere with shrill promises to a very tough manager to make the act bigger and better and blowsier than ever, there came an enormous trade-laugh. Klugman stepped in and amazingly succeeded in winning over the man. "Why did he listen to you?" asked a stunned Merman. Klugman patiently replied, "Oh, everybody in show business listens to *anybody*."

Merman was not the whole show, but she almost was, and beside her, Jack Klugman sounded adenoidal, while Sandra Church, with a delicate touch to her acting, had to really work at making her shy, retiring, juvenile Louise register vividly. Church's beauty worked to advantage, however, as did her emotional honesty, and she evoked a genuine response from Gypsy Rose Lee herself in the audience.

In the "Little Lamb" scene, when Louise sits alone in a tight spotlight at the corner of the otherwise darkened stage and sings to a lamb she has just received as a birthday gift, Gypsy was transported back to her childhood when her mother had made up stories to sustain her daughters when times were tough. She was also carried back to the times when she herself had invented stories for Erik to help them both stay awake through the long nights from date to date. They had been happy stories and comic ones, but her son had sensed a palpable sadness under all of them. Now art imitated life all too clearly, and Gypsy was on the verge of tears.

The first act seemed well balanced, because even though Merman was what Kenneth Tynan, writing in the *New Yorker* called "a nightmare incarnation of Noël Coward's Mrs. Worthington," Jack Klugman played Herbie with devoted restraint, and Sandra Church made young Louise a dewy-eyed, idealistic adolescent. Robbins's funny-awful vaudeville numbers, especially those with wildly posturing youngsters (all but drowned in American flags), were eye-catching and satirical, and Jacqueline Mayro's cavorting Baby June added wonderful comedy as she showed a mastery of effects, wearing a perennial mask of glee (even when no motive was apparent) or pretending a breathlessness after a not particularly exhausting routine. Merman did not score a knockout with any song, but she made all the lyrics count by her faultless enunciation, clarion tones, and shrewd body language. Her phrasing alone was worth the price of admission, and enlarged the character all by itself. "But I / At least gotta try" in "Some People" dragged out the "I" with such strong elasticity that she was thoroughly convincing as a woman who just had to get out of Seattle and away from "humdrum people." Merman's vibrato did not get in the way of the lyrics because it accentuated rather than overpowered the sense of Rose's wilfulness. In "You'll Never Get Away from Me," she used her body to seduce Klugman's Herbie, the travelling man who had just travelled into her overpowering orbit. Act 1 ended with Rose transferring her fantasies of fame for June onto Louise, as Sandra Church quailed and shook at her mother's beady stare. The character appeared to be guessing what was in store for her, and it was, Tynan wrote, "like watching a rabbit petrified by the headlights of a silently onrushing car."

At intermission, Gypsy and her son entered the lobby where she hoped to have a cigarette. However, she was surrounded by people who were anxious to congratulate her and she did not have a moment to herself. Not that she really minded in the least. Her eyes sparkled with pride even as she modestly paid tribute to the show's creators.

The second-half was a let-down for some — if for no other reason, according to Tynan, than the simple fact that "the effortless coalition" of all the arts of the American musical stage "at their highest point of development" could only be repeated, sometimes redundantly, and without the ability to disguise the fact that there was no solid male character or voice to counterbalance Merman, called by the *Newark Star-Journal* "a boiler-room in full operation." Some critics lamented the fact that one of the two heroines in the show had to be shunted aside, even though they recognized that Sandra Church's personality was not strong enough on its own to capture Gypsy's intrinsic animation even without competition from Merman. Robbins had never shown much faith in Church's ability to pull off her big strip number, but on the opening night, technical glitter made up for the actress' lack of sexy titillation. Her strip began with Church in a long-skirted, tight-fitting gray gown, which she did not remove. She merely stepped off stage and within seconds reappeared in a bright red dress cut along the same lines as its predecessor. This, too, remained on when she exited again. Then she reappeared in a bright blue dress, and it was hard to tell whether these were real costume changes or simply a clever illusion created by lighting. At any rate, the quick "changes" added a slick touch to the sequence. The text did not give much to the actress to work with, so what should have been one of the highest points in the evening became only moderately effective. But mild disappointment or disapproval over this portion of the show did not obscure Merman's extended brilliance. Her bright, trumpet voice built one peak after another in "Everything's Coming Up Roses," and many wondered just how high she could go. She used very few gestures — merely an arm movement or two, an upraised finger, some beats with the hands — but she was fully in control of the words and rhythm. Yet she wasn't singing for herself. By emphasizing the first word in the line "You'll be swell," she made it apparent that she was still dreaming for one of her daughters, and not for herself. She would, of course, swing around to her own outer and inner selves in the show-stopping "Rose's Turn," where she became a compendium of changing emphases and tones. When she announced at the top of her considerable voice: "HERE SHE IS, BOYS! HERE SHE IS, WORLD! HERE'S ROSE!!" nobody watching could remain uninvolved or unmoved. "You either got it, / or you ain't — / And, boys, I got it!" flaunted her soaring confidence in the garish neon setting which flashed her name "Rose" in electric lights. When she added a little bump and grind after performing part of June's act and then part of Louise's, she made it amply clear that she could have played the role of Gypsy herself some ten years or so earlier, had such a part been available to her. But the sung and spoken monologue gave her soul-searing flashes to set off. "Mama's got to let go" came like a lightning realization, followed by "Why did I do it?" with heavy bitterness in the reflection. And the full-throttled finish with "For me" repeated six times, always different in tone, made her breakdown spectacularly vulgar and explosive.

This number should have been enough to compensate for any other letdown in the second act, but some critics raised objections. Brooks Atkinson, for one, thought it one of the "sticky scenes" in the show and regretted the excursion into something more literary. "It deserts the body and starts cultivating the soul," he complained, as if one were automatically divided from the other. Others in a minority felt there were a few other faults in an otherwise superb show. According to Kenneth Tynan, the problems were manifold: one had to do with plot, because "having seen the grooming of Baby June," the audience now had to watch "the grooming of Gypsy," and this made for redundancy; the second was the fact that there were only three new songs — the rest were reprises; a third problem was the lack of "a good, solid male singer" ("Jack Klugman, the show's nearest approach to a hero, is an amiable actor, but his voice is no more than an amplified snore"); a fourth difficulty was that Sandra Church was "too chaste in demeanour to reproduce the guileful, unhurried carnality with which the real Gypsy undressed"; and the final problem was the finale, in which Merman interrupted her own "burlesque routine of staggering panache" in mid-phrase simply to lacerate herself in prose.

Nevertheless, even Tynan recognized that the second-half (which had "mere brilliance" in contrast to the "perfection" of the first act) did not obscure the fact that the overall "blending of skills," the precise "interlocking of song, speech, and drama" made "the sheer contemplation of technique" a thrilling emotional experience. Tynan's conclusive judgement was that the show made him feel as if he were present "at the triumphant solution of some harsh architectural problem" in which the finished structure seemed "as light as an exhalation, though in fact it [was] earthquake proof."

At show's end, Gypsy Rose Lee went backstage to see Merman to whom she had already sent a bouquet with a card reading, "Dear Ethel, How mother would have loved seeing you tonight. Love, Gypsy." She failed to notice, however, that her bouquet, along with every other well-wisher's, was placed in the corridor because Merman was allergic to flowers. Merman remembers that afterwards, Gypsy remarked to a reporter, "I told Ethel to drink lots of milk and stay healthy. She's going to be my annuity."

Among the host of greetings and good wishes that Merman received was a telegram which read: "DEAREST ETHEL, GLAD YOU ARE BACK AND IF YOU NEED AN UNDERSTUDY I KNOW WHERE YOU CAN GET ONE. GREAT GOOD LUCK FOR THE BIGGEST HIT EVER. LOVE, FREDDIE BRISSON." In her memoir, Merman remarked that this message might have given her shivers if she had possessed psychic powers, for Brisson was married to Rosalind Russell, the very person who would later steal the film role of Rose away from Merman.

The reviews from the major papers were sensational. Everybody received kudos — but particularly Merman, who was called everything from "trumpet-tonsiled" (*Time*) and "bugle-voiced" (*Herald Tribune*) to "the most relaxed brass section on earth" (Tynan) and "the busybody, the battleaxe, and the heart-breaking failure" all in one (Kerr). There were some complaints about Sandra Church's climactic strip number on a tank-town runway lit by a haze of footlights, though Walter Kerr appreciated the actress's reserve and "faltering delicacy" which ensured that "no trace of unspoken feeling" was lost. Every critic acknowledged the brilliant showmanship of the production, and everyone sang hosannas for Merman, especially in her finale when she stood alone in a neon-lit black box, "rhythmically stomping the earth as though she could make it give something back to her." As Kerr summed up after he had revisited the show a few nights later, "Miss Merman seems to have piled all her past successes together and to be standing on top of them."

And yet there was a shocker for the annals. The Tony Award for the Best Musical of the season was shared by *Fiorello!* and *The Sound of Music*, and *Gypsy* was shut out in the other categories as well. Jerome Robbins was nominated as Best Director, but lost to the legendary George Abbott (*Fiorello!*). Milton Rosenstock saw the Conductor and Musical Director Award go to Frederick Dvonch (*The Sound of Music*). Jo Mielziner lost out in the area of Scenic Design to Oliver Smith (*The Sound of Music*), and Raoul Pène du Bois had to be content with a nomination for Costume Design while the award went to Cecil Beaton (*Saratoga*). In the Supporting or Featured Actor category, Jack Klugman had no chance competing against Tom Bosley (*Fiorello!*), and Sandra Church saw Patricia Neway (*The Sound of Music*) walk off with the Supporting Actress prize. But the one category that should have been a shoo-in for *Gypsy* came up empty too — and that was the scandal of the whole affair. True, there was memorable competition in the Best Actress division, with Carol Burnett, Dolores Gray, Eileen Herlie, and Mary Martin all deserving of accolades, but surely the most unforgettable musical performance of the year — a truly legendary one — was Merman's, and she had already won the critics' poll, but she lost to her friend Mary Martin (*The Sound of Music*). When Cheryl Crawford attempted to offer condolences later, Merman cracked her up by shrugging: "How are you going to buck a nun?"

Since the American Theatre Wing had split the Best Musical award, a lot of people were up in arms against the committee for not splitting the Best Actress award. Merman, however, claimed not to care too much. She had been so confident about *Gypsy* that when she negotiated her contract in December 1958, she signed a year's lease at the Park Lane Hotel. Her show lasted 702 performances.

A Rose by Other Names

WELL-MEANING ADMIRERS of Merman demanded to know why their favourite was not appearing in the 1962 Mervyn LeRoy film version of *Gypsy*. Merman's answer was unwaveringly honest: "Nobody asked me." Freddie Brisson, the very one who had sent her the Broadway telegram offering her an eager understudy if she ever needed one, obviously thought that this "understudy" would do Rose better on celluloid than would Merman. He was biased, of course, because the "understudy" happened to be his own wife, Rosalind Russell. A business deal had already been struck between him and movie mogul Jack Warner. Brisson had purchased the screen rights to the Broadway hit *A Majority of One* for his wife and had agreed to allow Warner Brothers to produce it if the studio let Russell play Rose in *Gypsy*. Warner, who would later pick Audrey Hepburn over Julie Andrews for the film of *My Fair Lady*, preserved Hollywood's ignoble tradition of callously ignoring Broadway's original creators of hit roles. So Merman had her name added to a long list in this *salon de refusés*. It is true — as Ethan Mordden claims — that her early film roles were "all supporting parts as scheming molls or screwball friends," and failed to exploit her remarkable diction, pitch, and gutsy energy. Her earliest film roles, after she had become an instant Broadway star in *Girl Crazy*, were in Norman Taurog's *Follow the Leader* (1930), which starred Ed Wynn and Ginger Rogers, and as a romantic singer in a short, *Roaming* (1931), where she sang "Shake Well Before Using" and "Hello, My Lover, Good-bye." And when *Girl Crazy* was filmed in 1932, Kitty Kelly played a truncated version of Merman's role, while Merman sang and made a hit all over again of "I Got Rhythm."

In her great stage roles she was brassy and too tough for men.

Hollywood apparently did not think her qualities appropriate for its leading men, and even when she did get to play her Broadway roles in Paramount's *Anything Goes* (1936) and 20th Century-Fox's *Call Me Madam* (1953) — which had a strong cast that included Donald O'Connor, George Sanders, Billy De Wolfe, Walter Slezak, and Helmut Dantine — the studios diluted her parts so that she was "no longer right for them," according to Ethan Mordden in *The Hollywood Musical*. Except for Reno Sweeney and Sally Adams in the films just mentioned above, all her original roles went to movie stars: Ann Sothern was given *Panama Hattie*, Lucille Ball cut up in *Du Barry Was a Lady*, and Betty Hutton (replacing Judy Garland) inherited *Annie Get Your Gun*. With her omission from *Gypsy*, she was now a classic example of the shunned Broadway star.

There was a real scene when Merman first found out about Rosalind Russell. George Oppenheimer happened to be in Jule Styne's office the day Merman discovered that Brisson had engineered his wife's signing for Rose. Merman telephoned Styne and he turned white as she screamed out her fury. "Look, look, talk to George Oppenheimer," Styne begged in desperation. *"He'll* tell you the position I'm in." But Merman would not be so reasonable: "What the fuck do I want to talk to George Oppenheimer for? I want *you* to do something."

But nobody could do a thing after the big wheels in Hollywood were put in motion. Merman's disappointment was particularly acute because Rose was her favourite role, but when the movie was released in 1962 she could have consoled herself because the general critical opinion was that the film did not do the Broadway show justice. Pauline Kael called the movie "extremely unpleasant" and the direction "heavy and coarse." The critics were divided over Rosalind Russell. Everyone thought her too beautiful and not at all able to match Merman's clarion singing and faultless diction. But some film buffs — such as Ethan Mordden and Clive Hirschhorn — approved at times of her singular force of personality. She merely talked and whispered through "Some People," but she pulled off "You'll Never Get Away from Me" and pushed through "Everything's Coming Up Roses" after underlining her hurt and fury in the first line, "You'll . . . be . . . swell!" At times she still seemed to be battling to overcome her Auntie Mame image and so miscalculated some of her effects. At other times, aware that she had less volcanic power than Merman, she tried to capitalize on her superior screen acting, but she occasionally went over the top — rather like Auntie Mame auditioning for the Actors Studio.

It did not help matters that vulgarity appeared to be the signature of the film. Leonard Spigelgass's screenplay tried unsuccessfully to add depth and texture to Arthur Laurents's book, and while Mervyn LeRoy's recreation of a bygone theatrical era was accurate, it widened the burlesque scenes and lost some of the intimacy of the drama. The casting was uneven. Karl Malden was a credible Herbie, fraught with genuine concerns for Rose and Gypsy, and the strippers (Faith Dane, Betty Bruce, and Roxanne Arlen) were a standout in their raucous "You Gotta Have a Gimmick." But Natalie Wood seemed to act with her bottom, as some critics joked, although, ironically, she had the only moment which was superior to its equivalent in the stage show. This came when she was seen listening to the strippers as they sang and performed "You Gotta Have a Gimmick." She watched and listened attentively, and there was a glint in her eye as if at that very moment the great ecdysiast was being born. Stephen Sondheim singled out this scene as the one "really true and terrific moment" in a poor movie.

As if losing the film role were not enough, Merman also failed to do the British stage production, though this time it was chiefly by her own will. She did want to play Rose in London during the spring of 1962, but Jack Klugman was not able to go, and Julienne Marie (who had replaced Sandra Church as Louise — much to Merman's satisfaction) gave in to her husband's wish not to leave the country. Not wanting to do the production with a British cast, who probably would have been mismatched to the main roles, Merman forsook the opportunity to play London and signed, instead, for her Las Vegas début.

But she did go on tour with *Gypsy*, opening in Rochester on March 29, 1961, and playing Detroit, Cleveland, Boston, Toronto, Chicago, San Francisco, St. Louis, and Los Angeles. There were two significant cast changes: Julienne Marie was now playing Louise and was, Merman says, "much more professionally compatible" with Merman than was Sandra Church; and Betty Bruce was the new Tessie Tura and also Merman's understudy. Bruce had studied ballet as a child and had danced with the Metropolitan Opera corps de ballet before going to Broadway. She executed a fast ballet-like tap routine and showed a fine sense of humour offstage. Merman and she became friends.

In Boston, the production broke the ten-year-old box office record at the Colonial, and Merman remembers that she received a fan letter from Sir John Gielgud who claimed to have been one of her "most ardent fans" since *Annie Get Your Gun*. Gielgud wrote: "It was such a joy to sit once more at your feet and watch your incredibly simple and selective performance — not a superfluous gesture or elaboration. Yet you sway us with absolute certainty to whatever mood you wish to convey." Gielgud added that he thought her art comparable to that of Edith Evans, and exclaimed that America was indeed lucky to claim Merman and delight in her success.

After ten weeks in Chicago, the production moved to San Francisco, where she was greeted with a five-minute standing ovation before she even uttered her first line. She met with a similar reception nightly for eight weeks, and this adoring reaction motivated her to continue in the role even after she suffered excruciating pain with locked vertebrae. Merman was a genuine star who felt an obligation to the public as well as to the show itself. "Whether I hurt or not, I felt I had to go on. I couldn't let my co-workers down any more than I could let the audience down." David Merrick made a special visit to her and asked her to appear in *Hello, Dolly!* but she turned him down because she did not want to be connected to another long run so quickly.

The tour ended in St. Louis around Christmas. Official receipts showed that it had grossed $2,473,626.61. But there was more to come — without Merman. Several revivals were planned, though none materialized until 1971, when Fritz Holt (a young stage manager from Harold Prince's office) and Barry Brown (a music publishing executive) teamed up with two English partners to finance a British production. The English were starving for yet another Broadway musical. Indeed, at the charity benefit for *Funny Girl*, for which Styne did the music in 1966, Princess Margaret asked the composer, "When are you bringing *Gypsy* here?" The princess had to wait seven more years to have her wish fulfilled.

Ethel Merman was approached once again to star in the West End, and once again she declined. Both her parents were ill, and Taylor reports that she even rejected an offer by the producers to fly them to London and have them placed under special medical care there. Angela Lansbury was approached next and she, too, turned the offer down — although it was her own brother's idea to revive the show with her as Rose. Edgar Lansbury had produced *The Subject Was Roses*, *The Alchemist*, *Arms and the Man*, and *To Be Young, Gifted and Black*, and many others, but he had always wanted to produce a show starring his sister. He had first proposed the idea of Rose to her in 1969 but she was too intimidated by the memories and legend of Ethel Merman. Now, in late 1971, she was living on a farm in Ireland and busy solving family problems. She did not have much time or will to think about the stage, even though she had the depth of talent for the role, and she was a popular choice with Sondheim, Styne, and Bobby Tucker, a choreographer who had assisted Jerome Robbins in the original show and who was engaged to reproduce the show's dances and movements.

But Edgar and his partner, Joseph Beruh (producer of *Godspell*), did not give up. Elaine Stritch, a quirky but inspired comedienne, was dying to do Rose and after opening to great acclaim in the London version of *Company*, she was offered the part. However, her reputation was not enough to interest financial backers. The project seemed doomed — until Arthur Laurents's intervention. A trusted friend of Angela Lansbury ever since their collaboration on *Anyone Can Whistle* (1964), he urged her to re-read the script, and she suddenly discovered a new approach to the part. The ghost of Merman might still haunt the singing but not, probably, the acting. "If I occupy any rear seat at all in the theater," Lansbury once commented, "it is primarily as an actress, not as a musical personality." She knew full well that Merman had been all voice and musical power; she also knew that she could herself be all actress and dramatic truth.

Lansbury realized that *Gypsy* was really Rose's show, and that she could play her easily as a monster or a bitch. However, she wanted to play her quite differently. "*Gypsy* is really about a tragedy of good intentions," she revealed. "Rose is a pathetic person, but her guts make her rivetting, exciting, and extremely stage-worthy." She was still insecure about her musical ability, but her excitement over the new interpretation was enough to convince her to sign for the whole London run.

By the end of 1972, the young producers, lacking enough money of their own for an investment in the show, had raised all but $90,000 of the $275,000 budget. Lansbury put them in touch with her brother who, along with his partner Beruh, wrote out a cheque for the required amount. According to Theodore Taylor, Brown and Holt then booked the Picadilly Theatre, which was actually too small for a Broadway musical, and *Gypsy* was all set for a May opening in 1973, with Zan Charisse as Louise, Debbie Bowen as June, Barrie Ingham as Herbie, and Valerie Walsh, Kelly Wilson, and Judy Canon as the three strippers with a gimmick apiece.

Lansbury insisted on special four-week rehearsals with Styne prior to official production rehearsals. She wanted to know every note of the score before showing up in front of the full cast. When Styne began working with her, he knew within the first hour that he'd have a surprise for everyone. No one was certain about her singing. She was primarily an actress, and though she had sung in Sondheim's *Anyone Can Whistle* and had won a Tony for *Mame* in 1966 and another for *Dear World* three years later, there were special vocal and rhythmic requirements for *Gypsy*. By the end of the day, Styne knew that she'd be superb. "I let her have her own way. She began to act the pants off the part. Not as forceful as Merman, vocally not as blatant, but doing it a different way, her way." He called Holt, Sondheim, and Laurents who came over and were knocked over by her renditions of two songs — "Some People" and "Everything's Coming Up Roses."

She had to learn to forget about Merman — if such a thing was, indeed, possible. She had heard Merman sing the songs "countless times at parties," and she had met Merman shortly after signing to do the role.

"I hear you're going to do *Gypsy*," Merman said, never wanting to yield her territorial claim to Rose.

Lansbury relieved the tension. "Nobody but you can do *Gypsy*. But I'm going to have a go at it."

Luckily, she had never seen the original Broadway show, so she approached the part freshly, without predetermined technical choices. "I tried to find a core of honesty in the part, instead of playing a caricature of the stage mother."

Her Rose was a fully rounded character with a heart and soul and a mind that shattered with the disintegration of her personal and professional relationships. Laurents, who directed the revival, made several significant changes in the production which strengthened it. Sondheim added two new choruses for "Together, Wherever We Go," and Lansbury brought the house down as she danced. Dissatisfied with Gypsy's strip and the last scene between Gypsy and Rose, Laurents wrote additional lines for Gypsy. He had always wanted her to talk during her act because that's what Gypsy Rose Lee had done in her burlesque routines, but because Jerome Robbins never had much faith in Sandra Church's performance, this aspect was left out. But with Zan Charisse now playing Louise, the chatter worked, as the actress kept making repartée with her clothes on. Laurents gave her a few words of French: "*Bonsoir, messieurs. Je m'appelle Geepsee Rose Lee* . . . and that concludes my entire performance in French. I've been too busy learning Greek." Then she continued: "An ecdysiast is one who or that which sheds its skin — in vulgar parlance, a stripper. But I'm not a stripper. At these prices, I'm an ecdysiast." A little sexual suggestiveness, some wit, and always a varnish on the words and attitude. Not wholly up to Gypsy Rose Lee's own rhyming patter, but certainly good enough to convey aspects of her performing self and of a new confidence in burlesque wickedness and byplay. Audiences got a better sense of Louise's evolution as a woman, and the main pattern of the show became clearer. Originally, the second act had seemed weaker than the first, but in Laurents's production, the second act topped the first. The show became a genuine love story or really, a set of two love stories, for Rose now loved Herbie almost as much as she loved her own girls. When all three of her beloved ones left her, she was shattered and, so, the whole show built to "Rose's Turn."

In the original Broadway production, the audience applauded wildly as Merman did her bows after "Rose's Turn." Merman would then try not to bow and so get on with the play. And Sandra Church's Louise would appear from the wings and the audience would finally stop applauding. This was, as Sondheim saw it, a "standard way" of recovering from a show-stopper. However, in London, Laurents found a way of recovering without (in Sondheim's words) "violating the texture." He allowed Lansbury her knock-'em-down number with all stops out, but as the applause started to die, he had her continue bowing. Sondheim recalls: "There was dead silence in the house, and she kept bowing. You realized that you were looking at a mad woman, not at a musical."

Laurents appreciated Lansbury's courage. "When I asked her to do it, I hoped that the audience would realize this whole number is in her head, so that the applause also was in her head." The actress's risk was in continuing to bow even as the audience stopped applauding. She risked disdain for imagined egomania, but she performed so brilliantly that the audience realized that Rose was mad. Lansbury's Rose had a demented look in her eyes. On her third bow, all the lights that had spelled "Rose" above the proscenium went out, except for a spot on her. Then another spot picked up Gypsy as she walked on, while Rose kept bowing. At the end, when the two exited the stage (now lit only by a work light), Rose turned, in her daughter's fur coat, to look at the runway, and the lights started to come up. But when she looked at them, they went out. This signified that she was finished. A lonely, sad figure was passing into history. The stage seemed eerily cold as at a death, and a musical comedy had suddenly ended with a stunning mad scene.

At the final curtain, applause was tremendous. The cast received a fifteen-minute standing ovation. Lansbury had eleven curtain calls, during one of which she heard a voice cry from the balcony: "Welcome home!" She had left England thirty years earlier to make her reputation in Hollywood. Now on June 9, 1973, she was a returning expatriate celebrity. As the ovation continued, she stepped out of character to address the audience. "The night doesn't belong to me. It belongs to the authors, and you should meet them." Her humility and generosity startled Laurents, Sondheim, and Styne who "had never heard a star make that kind of speech on an opening-night curtain call," but they joined her on stage for their just public acknowledgement. Then they visited her backstage and rhapsodized: "We saw our show for the first time."

All London's theatre fans and critics were at Lansbury's feet. "Bow down, Bacall; Ethel Merman, you were not missed," gushed the *Daily Mail*. "The London musical stage belongs to only one woman from this very second; a rose by any other name is now Angela Lansbury." The normally acerbic Kenneth Tynan put aside his tartness to write: "In twenty years of London theater, I've never seen anything like this!" — forgetting for the while all the great English stage luminaries to whom he had paid inimitable homage.

Lansbury won the *Plays and Players* Award as Best Actress — the first time anyone had ever won for an appearance in a musical. Those who had seen Merman found Lansbury equally brilliant. Flora Roberts, Sondheim's agent, thought it unfair to compare the two performers, but summed the matter up by saying that "it was goose bumps with Merman and tears with Lansbury."

Gypsy, with Lansbury, Charisse, and a new American cast, began a full American tour in the spring of 1974 and then opened on Broadway on September 23, 1974, to rave reviews. Martin Gottfried exclaimed: "It's as if it had been born fresh, beautifully directed by Laurents." Clive Barnes called it a case of lightning striking twice, and added: "Everything about *Gypsy* is right. . . . [Lansbury] is enchanting, tragic, bewildering and bewildered. Miss Lansbury not only has a personality as big as the Statue of Liberty, but also a small core of nervousness that can make the outrageous real." And Walter Kerr, who thought that Merman and Lansbury were from "entirely different constellations," put Lansbury's achievement in proper perspective: "Miss Lansbury is not really to be compared to Miss Merman: there's no way of doing it. Miss Merman is a natural force, like the Colorado River. . . . Miss Lansbury is half fine actress, half ferocious personality, admirable because she works so hard and, in working so hard, works so honestly."

The verdict was in for posterity. There was a new star, a new name, but it was Rose's turn again.

Production Notes

Gypsy was first presented by David Merrick and Leland Hayward at the Broadway Theatre, New York, on May 21, 1959. The cast, in order of appearance, was as follows:

Uncle Jocko Mort Marshall

George Willy Sumner

Arnold (and accordion) Johnny Borden

Balloon Girl Jody Lane

Baby Louise Karen Moore

Baby June Jacqueline Mayro

Rose Ethel Merman

Pop Erv Harmon

Newsboys

Bobby Brownell   Gene Castle

Steve Curry   Billy Harris

Weber Joe Silver

Herbie Jack Klugman

Louise Sandra Church

June Lane Bradbury

Tulsa Paul Wallace

Yonkers David Winters

L.A. Michael Parks

Angie Ian Tucker

Kringelein Loney Lewis

Mr. Goldstone Mort Marshall

Miss Cratchitt Peg Murray

Farmboys

Marvin Arnold	Ricky Coll
Don Emmons	Michael Parks
Ian Tucker	Paul Wallace

David Winters

Cow Willy Sumner and George Zima

Pastey Richard Porter

Tessie Tura Maria Karnilova

Mazeppa Faith Dane

Cigar Loney Lewis

Electra Chotzi Foley

Showgirls

Kathryn Albertson	Denise McLaglen
Barbara London	Theda Nelson
Carroll Jo Towers	Marie Wallace

Renee Marsha Rivers

Phil Joe Silver

Bougeron-Cochon George Zima

Hollywood Blondes

Agnes Marilyn Cooper		*Thelma* Merle Letowt
Marjorie May Patsy Bruder		*Edna* Joan Petlak
Dolores Marilyn D'Honau		*Gail* Linda Donovan

Entire production directed and
choreographed *by* Jerome Robbins
Settings and lighting *by* Jo Mielziner
Costumes designed *by* Raoul Pène du Bois
Musical direction *by* Milton Rosenstock
Orchestrations *by* Sid Ramin with Robert Ginzler
Dance music arranged *by* John Kander
Additional dance music *by* Betty Walberg

Works Consulted

Alpert, Hollis. *Broadway! 125 Years of Musical Theatre*. New York: Arcade/ Little, Brown, 1991.

Amberg, George. *Ballet: The Emergence of an American Art*. New York: Mentor, 1951.

Arnold, Elliott. "The Young Idea." *New York World-Telegram* 27 Apr. 1940.

Aston, Frank. " 'Gypsy,' Ethel Smash Hits." *New York World-Telegram and Sun*, 22 May 1959.

Atkinson, Brooks. "Good Show!" *New York Times* 22 May 1959.

Beckerman, Bernard, and Howard Siegman, eds. *On Stage: Selected Theater Reviews from The New York Times 1920–1970*. New York: Arno, 1973.

Bordman, Gerald. *American Musical Comedy: From "Adonis" to "Dreamgirls."* New York: Oxford UP, 1982.

———. *American Musical Theatre*. New York: Oxford UP, 1986.

———. *The Concise Oxford Companion to American Theatre*. New York: Oxford UP, 1987.

Chapman, John. "Miss Merman Has Her Best Role in 'Gypsy,' a Real-Life Musical." *New York Daily News* 22 May 1959.

Coleman, Emily. "From Tutus to T-Shirts." *New York Times Magazine* 8 Oct. 1961.

Coleman, Robert. " 'Gypsy' a Dynamic Musical." *New York Daily Mirror* 1959.

Engel, Lehman. *Their Words Are Music: The Great Theatre Lyricists and Their Lyrics*. New York: Crown, 1975.

———. *This Bright Day: An Autobiography*. New York: Macmillan, 1974.

———. *Words with Music: The Broadway Musical Libretto*. New York: Schirmer, 1972.

"Ethel Merman Aglow." Rev. of *Gypsy. Newsweek* 1 June 1959.

Ewen, David. *Complete Book of the American Musical Theater*. New York: Holt, 1959.

Gaghan, Jerry. " 'Gypsy' No Grind with Merman as Stripper's Mom." *Philadelphia Daily News* 14 Apr. 1959.

Gottfried, Martin. *Broadway Musicals*. New York: Abrams, 1979.

Green, Stanley. *Encyclopedia of the Musical Theatre*. New York: Da Capo, 1976.

———. *The World of Musical Comedy*. New York: Barnes, 1974.

Guernsey, Jr., Otis L., ed. *Broadway Song & Story: Playwrights/Lyricists/ Composers Discuss Their Hits*. New York: Dodd, Mead, 1985.

———. *Curtain Time: The New York Theater 1965–1987*. New York: Applause Theatre Books, 1987.

Harris, Radie. "Broadway Ballyhoo." *Hollywood Reporter* 26 May 1959.

Havoc, June. *Early Havoc*. London: Hutchinson, 1960.

———. *More Havoc*. New York: Harper, 1980.

Hirschhorn, Clive. *The Hollywood Musical*. London: Octopus, 1981.

"His Words Are Music to Our Ears." *Newsday* 14 Dec. 1987.

Holt, Georgia, and Phyllis Quinn, with Sue Russell. *Star Mothers: The Moms Behind the Celebrities*. New York: Simon, 1988.

Jackson, Arthur. *The Best Musical: From "Show Boat" to "A Chorus Line."* Foreword Clive Barnes. New York: Crown, 1977.

Kael, Pauline. *5001 Nights at the Movies: A Guide from A to Z*. New York: Holt, 1982.

Kasha, Al, and Joel Hirschhorn. *Notes on Broadway: Intimate Conversations with Broadway's Greatest Songwriters*. New York: Fireside, 1987.

Kerr, Walter. " 'Gypsy.' " *New York Herald Tribune* 22 May 1959.

———. *Journey to the Center of the Theater*. New York: Knopf, 1979.

———. *The Theater in Spite of Itself*. New York: Simon, 1963.

———. "Vigorous, Fresh, Stubborn 'Gypsy.' " *New York Herald Tribune* 31 May 1959.

Kislan, Richard. *Hoofing on Broadway: A History of Show Dancing*. New York: Prentice, 1987.

Laurents, Arthur. *Gypsy: Great Musicals of the American Theatre, Volume One*. Ed., introd., and notes by Stanley Richards. Radnor, PA: Chilton, 1973.

Lee, Gypsy Rose. *Gypsy: A Memoir*. New York: Fireside, 1986.

Lerner, Alan Jay. *The Musical Theatre: A Celebration*. London: Collins, 1986.

Longwood, William. "Chance of a Spot in 'Gypsy' Teases Strippers' Ambitions." *New York World-Telegram and Sun* 20 Jan. 1959.

McClain, John. "Huge Night for Merman and Her Fans." *Journal American* 22 May 1959.

Mielziner, Jo. *Designing for the Theatre: A Memoir and a Portfolio*. New York: Atheneum, 1965.

Mordden, Ethan. *Broadway Babies: The People Who Made the American Musical*. New York: Oxford UP, 1983.

———. *The Hollywood Musical*. New York: St. Martin's, 1981.

Morehouse, Ward. " 'Gypsy' a Romp for Merman and the Audience as Well." *Newark Star Journal* 23 June 1959.

Murdock, Henry T. "Ethel Merman Is Back." *Philadelphia Inquirer* 5 Apr. 1959.

Nelson, Don. "Laurents: Still the Same Old 'Story.' " *New York Daily News* 15 Feb. 1980.

"New Musical on Broadway." Rev. of *Gypsy*. *Time* 1 June 1959.

Preminger, Erik Lee. *Gypsy & Me: At Home and on the Road with Gypsy Rose Lee*. Boston: Little, 1984.

Ross, Dan. "Bugle-Voiced Ethel Turns to Acting." *New York Herald Tribune* 17 May 1959.

Rothstein, Mervyn. "Man Behind 'Gypsy' Prefers Now to Then." *New York Times* 15 Jan. 1990.

Schier, Ernie. " 'Gypsy' Brings Merman to Shubert Stage." *Philadelphia Evening Bulletin* 14 Apr. 1959.

"Stage Designer Finds Junkman Is Least of Hollywood's Worries." *New York Herald Tribune* 21 Dec. 1941.

Suskin, Steven. *Opening Night on Broadway*. New York: Schirmer, 1990.

Swados, Elizabeth. *Listening Out Loud: Becoming a Composer*. New York: Harper, 1989.

Swain, Joseph P. *The Broadway Musical: A Critical and Musical Survey*. New York: Oxford UP, 1990.

Taubman, Howard. *The Making of the American Theatre*. New York: Coward, 1965.

Taylor, Theodore. *Jule: The Story of Composer Jule Styne*. New York: Random, 1979.

Terry, Walter. "Robbins' First Love." *New York Herald Tribune* 8 Oct. 1961.

Todd, Michael, Jr., and Susan McCarthy Todd. *A Valuable Property: The Life Story of Michael Todd*. New York: Arbor, 1983.

Tynan, Kenneth. "Cornucopia." Rev. of *Gypsy*. *New Yorker* 30 May 1959.

Wander, Margaret. *Angela Lansbury: A Biography*. Bonanno, NY: St. Martin's, 1987.

Watts, Jr., Richard. "Ethel Merman Has Another Success." *New York Post* 22 May 1959.

Welles, Benjamin. "Raoul Pene du Bois." *New York Times* 8 Sept. 1940.

White, Mark. " '*You Must Remember This* . . .': *Popular Songwriters 1900–1980.* London: Warne, 1983.

Wiley, Mason, and Damien Bona. *Inside Oscar: The Unofficial History of the Academy Awards.* New York: Ballantine, 1987.

Wilk, Max. *They're Playing Our Song.* New York: Atheneum, 1973.

Wilson, Barbara L. "Fable Is Label for 'Gypsy.' " *Philadelphia Inquirer* 5 Apr. 1959.

"Wynn Costume Designer Scoffs at Modesty." *New York World-Telegram* 18 Dec. 1937.

Zadan, Craig. *Sondheim & Co.* New York: Harper, 1989.

Printed in Canada